Photovoltaic Power Systems
for Inspectors & Plan Reviewers

About the author

John Wiles is perhaps the most recognized name in the solar industry for his tremendous contribution to the development of codes and code compliance for PV. He has written hundreds of articles on code-related, photovoltaic system topics and is a regular contributor to *IAEI* magazine.

Wiles retired from his full-time position as a research engineer at the Southwest Technology Development Institute at New Mexico State University on February 28, 2013 after 24 years in the position. He continues to work there 25% of his time to keep active in the codes and standards development process, to assist inspectors and plan reviewers with code questions, to make "PV and the *NEC*" presentations throughout the country and to consult with the PV Industry on code-related issues.

He is a member of several of the Standards Technical Panels (STP) for Underwriters Laboratories (UL) and is active in formulating standards for PV equipment such as modules, inverters, charge controllers, combiners, cables, racks and connectors. He continues to write the "Perspectives on PV " articles in the *IAEI News* and is active in the development of proposals for the 2017 *NEC*.

As an old solar pioneer, he lived for 16 years in a stand-alone, off-grid PV-powered home in suburbia. His new owner-designed and built retirement home has a 7.5 kW utility-interactive PV system with whole house battery back up where he lives with his wife Patti, three dogs and two cats.

This work was supported by the United States Department of Energy under Contract DE-FC 36-05-G015149

Photovoltaic Power Systems for Inspectors & Plan Reviewers

Second Edition

John Wiles

International Association of Electrical Inspectors
Richardson, Texas

Published 2012, 2014 by
International Association of Electrical Inspectors
901 Waterfall Way, Suite 602
Richardson, TX 75080-7702

Copyright © 2012, 2014 by John Wiles

All rights reserved. First Edition published June 2012.
Printed in the United States of America
18 17 16 15 14   5 4 3 2 1

ISBN-10: 1-890659-70-3
ISBN-13: 978-1-890659-70-7

Photos used in this book were shot in situ or at tradeshows.
Use of the photos does not imply endorsement by IAEI
of the manufacturers or the products.

The material in this book has been extracted from and expanded upon the series of articles "Perspectives on PV" found in *IAEI News* published by the International Association of Electrical Inspectors. The articles are based on the author's understanding of the 2005, 2008, 2011, and 2014 *National Electrical Code*, his activities in developing that *Code*, his design reviews, inspections and testing of PV systems for more than twenty years, and his interaction with electrical inspectors, PV systems designers, and PV installers throughout the country. In all cases, the *NEC* is the requirement and local AHJs provide the interpretations of the *Code*.

DISCLAIMER

This book provides information on how the 2005, 2008, 2011, and 2014 *National Electrical Codes (NEC)* apply to photovoltaic systems. The book is not intended to supplant or replace the *NEC*; it paraphrases the *NEC* where it pertains to photovoltaic systems and should be used with the full text of the *NEC*. Users of this book should be thoroughly familiar with the *NEC* and know the engineering principles and hazards associated with electrical and photovoltaic power systems. The information in this book is the best available at the time of publication and is believed to be technically accurate. Application of this information and results obtained are the responsibility of the user.

In most locations, all electrical wiring including photovoltaic power systems must be accomplished by, or under the supervision of a licensed electrician and then inspected by a designated local authority. Some municipalities have additional codes that supplement or replace the *NEC*. The local inspector has the final say on what is acceptable.

This book has not been processed in accordance with NFPA Regulations Governing Committee Projects. Therefore, the text and commentary in it shall not be considered the official position of the NFPA or any of its committees and shall not be considered to be, nor relied upon as a formal interpretation of the meaning or intent of any specific provision or provisions of the 2005, 2008, 2011, or 2014 editions of NFPA 70, *National Electrical Code*.[1]

Author and the publisher do not warrant or guarantee any of the products described herein nor have they performed any independent analysis in connection with any of the product information contained herein. Publisher does not assume, and expressly disclaims, any obligation to obtain and include information referenced in this work.

The reader is expressly warned to consider carefully and adopt all safety precautions that might be indicated by the activities described herein and to avoid all potential hazards. By following the instructions contained herein, the reader willingly assumes all risks in connection with such instructions.

THE AUTHOR AND THE PUBLISHER MAKE NO REPRESENTATIONS OR WARRANTIES OF ANY KIND, INCLUDING, BUT NOT LIMITED TO, THE IMPLIED WARRANTIES OF FITNESS FOR PARTICULAR PURPOSE, MERCHANTABILITY OR NON-INFRINGEMENT, NOR ARE ANY SUCH REPRESENTATIONS IMPLIED WITH RESPECT TO SUCH MATERIAL. THE AUTHOR AND THE PUBLISHER SHALL NOT BE LIABLE FOR ANY SPECIAL, INCIDENTAL, CONSEQUENTIAL OR EXEMPLARY DAMAGES RESULTING, IN WHOLE OR IN PART, FROM THE READER'S USES OF OR RELIANCE UPON THIS MATERIAL.

[1] *National Electrical Code* and *NEC* are registered trademarks of the National Fire Protection Association, Inc., Quincy, MA 02169

Table of Contents

Preface 9

Part 1 Photovoltaic Power Systems

1 Changes and Challenges 11

2 An Overview of PV Systems 18

3 PV Modules Are Weird Beasts 27

4 Connecting the Module to Mother Earth 36

5 PV Modules 43

6 Still on the Roof 49

7 Details, Details, Details 57

8 The Inverter — Operation and Connections 65

9 Grounding the Inverter and the PV Array 72

10 Load-Side AC Utility Connections 79

11 Supply-Side PV Utility Connections 87

12 The Microinverter, the AC PV Module and DC-to-DC Converters 96

13 Plan Checking and Inspecting 103

14 The 15-Minute PV Inspection — Can You? Should You? 111

Part 2 Appendices

A   PV Math   118

B   Connecting and Wiring Microinverters and AC PV Modules   122

C   Grounding PV Modules   127

D   Conductor Sizing and Overcurrent Device Ratings   130

E   690.64(B)(2) / 705.12(D)(2) Load-Side Connections for Utility-Interactive PV Inverter   135

F   Fusing of DC PV Module Circuits in Utility-Interactive PV Systems   137

G   2005 / 2008 / 2011 *NEC* Photovoltaic Electrical Power Systems Inspector/Installer Checklist   143

H   Load-Side PV Connections, 705.12(D) in the 2014 *NEC*   148

I   2014 *NEC* Photovoltaic Electrical Power Systems Inspector/Installer Checklist   154

J   A Brief Overview: PV and the 2014 *National Electrical Code*   160

Part 3   Index

Photovoltaic

Power becomes more of our renewable energy source daily

Residential systems

Commercial systems

Industrial systems

Lighthouses

Navigation systems

Batteries

Electric vehicles

Power stations

Water pumps

Emergency telephones

Speed detectors

Traffic signs

Satellite systems

Street lights

Power tools

Indoor lighting

Photovoltaic Power Systems

Preface

In a time where photovoltaic plan reviewers and inspectors are getting pressured to expedite the inspection and review process, this document could not have come at a better time. If we are expected to accomplish quicker turnaround times with fewer inspections, we must be informed to insure safe/code-compliant installations. Rubber-stamping plans and drive-by inspections may be what the industry is pushing for, but are those actions what the customer deserves? The customer is relying upon qualified inspectors to verify that the PV system is safe and that it will continue to be safe for years of operation.

What makes this document stand out is how it correlates to the *National Electrical Code* (*NEC*). When citing corrections or comments, we need to be able to reference the *Code* to justify our call. The last thing that we should be doing is trying to enforce our opinion.

Stamping a set of PV drawings for approval or signing a permit card for an inspection does not require skill or knowledge of *NEC* requirements we need. The knowledge and skill *before* we sign or stamp documents is where most of us need some help and guidance. Having a document such as *Photovoltaic Power Systems* provides inspectors a great tool for gathering information on what to look for in plan review and during an inspection.

Article 690 is a small section when compared to the entire *NEC*. The size of Article 690 does not make it any less important than any other articles found in the *NEC*. Due to its size, it is often not a focus of the combination inspector. It is no wonder it gets overlooked when you stack up all the codes the combination inspector must enforce.

When the *NEC* book and handbook are not enough to help you understand what or how you should be enforcing the regulations, this document can provide clarity. The information provided in this document has been compiled by someone who is known throughout the industry as a PV expert. John Wiles has been a resource and has been providing training for over 20 years to inspectors and plan reviewers.

Not only is this document based on the current 2011 *Code* and earlier editions, but also the upcoming 2014 *NEC*. In the sidebars and Appendix H, you can see what is coming up in the next code cycle. With knowledge comes credibility. This document will help plan reviewers and inspectors know and understand what they are looking at and what to look for. If you want to understand what is on the plans, this document will help. Even for those who have a solid understanding of PV, it is helpful to have a document to refer to in times of question. Whether the question comes from us or from the PV designer or installer, this document can help answer these PV related questions.

You will find this document to be an excellent resource if you take the time to read it.

Having ready access to this document can help us all be more informed about PV, where expertise is often limited. John Wiles is known for having such expertise.

— Rhonda Parkhurst
Electrical Specialist
City of Palo Alto, California

Chapter 1
Changes and Challenges

For nearly a century from about 1897 to 1997, premises wiring systems in residences and commercial buildings have largely been collections of passive conductors, disconnects and overcurrent devices. Certainly there have been incremental improvements in these systems and they can be quite complex with the addition of transformers, motor controllers, GFCIs and AFCIs, but much of that complexity is due to the connected loads that are not covered in inspections under the requirements of the *National Electrical Code (NEC)*.

In 1997, interactive power sources such as photovoltaic (PV) power systems started being installed in large numbers due to financial incentives in California and elsewhere. PV systems were just the start of a parade of technology changes that will affect large segments of the electrical power distribution and premises wiring systems, and the inspection requirements for those systems.

The Changes

Electric Vehicles

We now have both plug-in hybrid electrical cars (PHEV) (fueled engines plus electric motors and batteries) and pure electric cars (EV) (electric motors and batteries) that require charging stations at not only the home base of such cars, but also in locations throughout the area that these vehicles will roam. Like cell phone coverage, the charging stations will be concentrated in metropolitan areas and then spread to less populated areas as the demand for extended coverage grows. Owners of these electric vehicles will certainly have charging stations in their homes and probably at their job sites. At the very least, there will be a new type of receptacle outlet to deal with and probably relatively high current branch circuits.

Plans are also being made to have parked, fully charged electric vehicles feed some of the energy stored in the on-board battery bank back into the utility grid at peak demand times. To control this exchange of energy from grid to car and back, and to ensure that the car is ready and charged when needed, will require communication between the car, the owner, and the utility. Such communication links may be wireless, over the Internet or through a hardwired connection along with the power connections. Like utility-interactive PV systems, these vehicle storage systems will require new code

PHOTO 1.1 Electric car

Chapter 1 — Changes and Challenges   11

changes and additional inspections to ensure public safety.

Large Energy Storage Systems

The utilities will embrace the dispatchable energy storage and generation systems. They will be able to tap energy that has been stored or that is available throughout the distribution network for use to offset peak demand loads. This operation will avoid having to increase the size of already taxed power plants and transmission lines. Backup generators at hospitals and other locations are already being used in this mode of operation. These emergency power systems are leased, operated and maintained by third parties who run them when not needed for emergencies and sell the power to the utilities during peak load periods.

Flow batteries are coming to the market. These batteries use stored liquid chemicals in a process that yields a very long-lived battery that can be rapidly charged and deeply discharged virtually an unlimited number of times. The batteries will be charged and energy will be stored during off peak demand periods and released back into the grid during peak demand times. Of course, the process will require utility-interactive systems to interface with the utility grid and communications systems to control the process. These systems and fuel cells (*NEC* Article 692) operating from natural gas will probably first appear in commercial buildings that have the necessary space. These systems will either be leased or owned, but in most cases, these new technology systems will require permitting and inspections of the added mechanical systems, the utility-interactive electrical connections and the communication circuits.

The Smart Grid

Energy demands throughout the country, and the world, are increasing steadily and will necessitate some combination of increasing the supply from new generation plants (coal, gas, oil or nuclear and renewable), reducing the demand through conservation, or restructuring of the existing distribution and consumption system. The infrastructure of utility generation and distribution systems is fairly robust, but very old, and somewhat inflexible in dealing with increased use of distributed energy sources and the issues associated with moving power from the sources to the consumers in other areas. The Smart Grid programs are designed to modernize the entire system from the generation plant to the end-use load.

Although many see the term *Smart Grid* and think that it will not impact the premises wiring, the *NEC*, or the inspection process, that would be

PHOTO 1.2 The infrastructure of utility generation and distribution systems is fairly robust, but very old, and somewhat inflexible in dealing with increased use of energy sources and the associated issues. Smart Grid programs are designed to modernize the entire system from the generation plant to end-use load.

PHOTO 1.3 Small wind system combined with solar panels

a misconception. At the present time utilities are installing smart meters as rapidly as they can find funds to do so. These smart meters are computer (microprocessor) based and not only allow remote reading and power quality recording (real power, reactive power, power factor and more), but may also serve as the interface between the smart grid and the smart house. Some of the smart meters even have the ability to allow the power to be remotely disconnected when bills are not paid.

The smart house will soon become a reality. Appliance manufacturers are already making dishwashers, clothes washers and other appliances that communicate through either hardwired or wireless communication systems to the smart meter and then to the utility. When financially beneficial to the consumer, or possibly when legislated, these smart appliances will be remotely controlled (by the utility) so that they may be operated only during times of low demand on the utility system. Those appliances may have unique plugs and receptacles and possibly communication connections. All of those new load connections must be inspected, of course.

What will be the impact on the *Code* of a house that does have load circuits and loads that may be remotely controlled or managed? How will service, feeder, and branch circuit sizes be determined? Copper conductor prices may rise so high that we are forced to control power flow so that smaller conductors can be used. Eventually, the use of electricity on the premises may be scheduled so that the maximum current ever drawn may be significantly less than that requiring a 100- or 200-amp service today. Smaller conductors and circuit sizes may reduce the ever-increasing costs of electrical installations, but *Code* revisions would be needed. With the demise of the incandescent light bulb do we really need three volt-amps per square foot for general-purpose circuits? Oh yes, there will be those 100+ inch flat panel displays on all four walls to deal with.

Is DC coming back?
Then we have the new trend of going back to direct current end-use appliances. Most electronic appliances such as cell phone chargers, radios, TVs, DVRs, DVD players, cable boxes, satellite receivers, track lighting and the like, while being plugged into a 120-volt ac receptacle outlet, actually run on low-voltage direct current (dc). Fluorescent and LED lighting bulbs and fixtures also operate on direct current. Significant losses are incurred to transforming the 120-volt ac line voltage into low voltage dc.

At the present time, dc lighting fixtures are being installed in commercial buildings and are being powered during the day directly from photovoltaic (PV) power systems with no conversion to ac until the electronic ballasts are reached. Solar lighting power is supplemented with utility power when necessary.

With the reduction of use of the incandescent light bulb over the next few years, the return of low-voltage dc power distribution systems for lighting and electronics is almost a certainty. Shades of the 1970s and 1980s! Maybe those off-grid long-haired solar hippies who insisted on staying with the 12-volt dc PV systems and electrical systems in their homes were far ahead of their time! Of course, appliances needing significant power for heat or mechanical motion like ranges, clothes washers, toasters, water heaters and the like will usually need higher voltages to keep the current and hence

Chapter 1 — Changes and Challenges

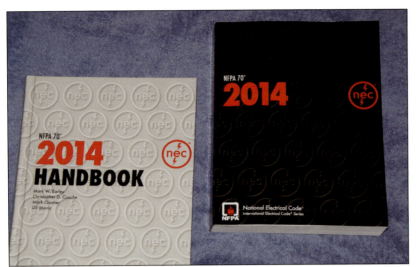

PHOTO 1.4 Codes and standards are racing to keep up with the new systems and devices.

the conductor sizes to reasonable sizes. But then we do have heat pump water heaters, induction ranges, and ultrasonic washers that operate more efficiently than conventional appliances.

Renewable Energy Systems

Large wind power systems have been installed for many years and many of those systems are not owned and operated by utilities on utility property. They therefore come under the requirements of the *NEC* and should be inspected for safety even though the 2011 *NEC* does not have a large wind system article. Article 694 has been added to the *Code* for wind systems, and UL has standards for large and small wind turbines. Photovoltaic power systems for residential and commercial use have been around since the mid-1970s with substantial growth starting in the late 1990s.

While ever-increasing numbers of residential and small PV systems are being installed throughout the country, real power production will come from the numerous megawatt commercial systems being installed and planned. Systems as large as 550 megawatts are being planned and installed and some of these will be solar thermal systems along with the PV systems. In many cases, these large systems are said to be "Behind the Fence" and not subject to the requirements of the *NEC* and inspections, but in reality, they are mainly owned and operated by private companies under power purchase agreements (PPA) and should be fully *NEC* compliant.

True AC PV modules with microinverters bonded to the back of the PV module with no dc wiring are appearing on the market in catalogs and in big box stores at impulse-buying prices. Will these products be listed? Will these be permitted? Will they be installed by qualified persons (those having the skills, training, and experience) [690.4(E), *NEC*-2011]? Will they be installed on dedicated circuits that will ensure public safety? Or will they be plugged into the nearest GFCI outlet and abuse the *Code* and safety in many ways?

DC-to-DC converters attached to or connected to PV modules are appearing on the market along with matching inverters in some cases. The *NEC* does not specifically give guidance on how to deal with them and future editions of the *Code* may show a similar trend.

All of these changing and emerging technologies will create challenges for the inspectors and plan reviewers and also an opportunity to excel.

The Challenges

Electrical inspectors, plan reviewers and combination inspectors are being challenged today and for the foreseeable future with all of these new and evolving energy production and storage sources that will be in use throughout the country. Many of them will appear connected to premises wiring and they will come under the requirements of the *NEC*. Many of those multi-megawatt PV, wind, and solar electric farms will fall under the *Code*.

The Code

Each edition of the *NEC* is developed over a three-year period through the code-making process that is well established. Competent, experienced volunteers make up the code-making panels (CMP) and with the NFPA/NEC Technical Correlating Committee (volunteers and professional staff) review and evaluate thousands of proposals and comments on proposals submitted from numerous sources. There are only two week-long (or less) meetings over that three-year cycle where the CMPs develop and write the *Code*.

With electrical and electronic technologies changing at a rapid pace, it is unreasonable to expect the *NEC* to keep abreast of all of the newest tech-

Looking forward to 2014

New and Unusual Challenge. Although not addressed by the 2014 *Code*, a new challenge has emerged that will certainly be of great interest to inspectors, plan reviewers, utility companies, certifying/listing agencies, and the mainstream PV industry.

This challenge is the proliferation of "Plug-And-Play" PV systems. These systems are being sold to the general public through the Internet and some retail outlets. The systems use creative advertisements including language like Underwriters Laboratories (UL) "approved" components and tout the ease of installation for anyone. Most claim that the unit can be installed and just plugged in to nearest ac electrical outlet by the homeowner. There are allusions to the fact that these systems can be purchased and plugged in with no electrical permit or inspection required and no contact with the local utilities.

An examination of existing descriptions of the systems reveal that there are probably numerous code violations and violations of the Underwriters Laboratories standards involved with the equipment. Although, the micro-inverters being used may be listed and the PV modules may be listed, the micro-inverters are not listed for use with standard AC plug connections and the exposed male blades on a standard NEMA plug will represent a safety hazard. The PV module may be mounted and grounded in a manner that is not consistent with its listing. And of course, backfeeding a standard receptacle outlet on a typical 15 or 20 amp branch circuit would violate several code requirements.

Additions. Part X was added to Article 690 and it addresses requirements for charging electric vehicles with PV systems and refers to Article 625. Section 690.91 may impose some restrictions on the PV system for charging electric vehicles if the maximum system voltage is above 80 V.

nologies that appear in the marketplace, even though the volunteers and staff make a valiant effort to do so. Many of those technologies are changing in form and function on a monthly basis and are not addressed by the *Code*, even though they are listed and certified under appropriate standards and are in the market place.

The Standards

Underwriters Laboratories and other organizations are developing safety standards as rapidly as possible. However, the development and revision process for standards and the harmonization of U. S. standards with those from Europe can and does take long periods of time. Those periods can even exceed the three-year cycle of the *NEC*.

Although the *NEC* and the UL Standards are intended to be used together to achieve an essentially hazard-free electrical installation, there are sometimes gaps between the two due to the lengthy revision processes and the emergence of new technologies. For example, the *2011 NEC*, adopted by some jurisdictions on January 1, 2011, has a requirement for a DC PV arc-fault detection and interruption system in Section 690.11, but there was no current UL Standard as of January 2011 that covers the safety evaluation of such a device. And the DC PV AFCI devices were already in the market. UL Standard 1699B is now available.

Continuing Education and Information

The challenge for every electrical inspector and plan reviewer is to keep abreast of these new developments as they start to appear in residential, commercial, and industrial electrical systems. The inspectors and the plan reviewers need to know as much, or more, about these new devices and systems as the people installing them. That has been true in the past and it needs to be the standard of performance in the future if the inspection community is to ensure the safety of the public.

Where the *Code* and the standards cannot keep up with these new systems and devices, the inspector and plan reviewer must devote time to educate themselves on the systems that they are and will be inspecting. Strong continuing education programs for the inspectors and plan reviewers must be a part of the planning in every jurisdiction. Time and funding must be budgeted for classes, for webinars, for technical documents, and for the equipment needed

PHOTO 1.5 Digital cameras and transmission of on-site pictures will become the inspectors tools.

to efficiently and proficiently review and inspect these ever-changing electrical power systems.

The inspectors and plan reviewers should have electronic copies of all codes, handbooks for those codes, and technical data (including manuals and specification sheets) for all types of systems being inspected and for equipment that may be installed on those systems. Laptop computers (with screens that can be read outdoors) with this information (updated as necessary) should accompany each inspector as the field inspections are conducted. Communication between the inspectors and the plan reviewers on a real-time basis via cell phone and wireless computer link will be required. Digital cameras, downloads and transmission of on-site pictures will become necessary.

Inspectors and plan reviewers are professionals today and will remain professionals in the eyes of the public as they rise to the challenges presented by the changes in the electrical power system today and tomorrow.

This book is intended to help inspectors, plan reviewers and installers keep abreast of the rapidly changing *NEC* requirements for the installation of photovoltaic power systems.

Resources

There are many resources available to the inspector and plan reviewer. Most equipment manufacturers have electronic downloadable PDF files of all manuals that will be useful. Here are a few magazines (available in print and on the web) that will enable inspectors and plan reviewers to keep abreast of the changing technologies.

IAEI News. http://www.iaei.org/magazine

Solar Pro. http://www.solarprofessional.com

Home Power. http://www.homepower.com

Solar Today. http://www.ases.org

The direct current portions of the PV system coupled with the alternating current interconnection to the utility grid make PV installations somewhat unique.

Chapter 2
An Overview of PV Systems

Photovoltaic (solar electric) power systems will be one solution to the nation's energy crisis brought upon us by dependence on foreign oil supplies.

Photovoltaic (PV) power systems are being installed by the tens of thousands throughout the United States. In states like California, New York, New Jersey and others where financial incentives are available, the PV business is booming. The first PV cells produced nearly 50 years ago are still producing power, and modern PV modules are expected to produce energy for the next 40 years or longer. The power output from PV systems ranges from a few hundred watts to many megawatts. Most of the systems are *not* operated or owned by any electric utility and therefore come under the requirements of the *National Electrical Code* (*NEC*). Systems as large as 200 megawatts have been installed by third parties on private land, and are not under utility control or ownership. Larger systems are being planned. These systems operate at 600 volts and higher and, in the larger commercial systems, the dc and ac currents can range up to 2000 amps or more. These levels of voltage and current, if not properly managed, pose shock, life safety and fire hazards. They must be inspected to ensure the safety of the owners, operators, service personnel, and the public.

The *Code* requirements for a typical residential PV system are at least as complex as those for residential wiring, and the direct current (dc) portions of the system coupled with the alternating current (ac) interconnection to the utility grid make PV installations somewhat unique. Because the PV industry is thriving and growing rapidly, individuals, companies, and organizations with varying degrees of knowledge, skill, and experience are installing these systems. Large (and some small) PV systems integrators and vendors working with experienced electrical contractors who have jointly pursued additional PV-specific training and who work closely with the local permitting and inspecting authorities usually (but not always) perform the best, most code-compliant installations.

On the other hand, individuals or organizations that have little or no experience or training in installing electrical systems of any type are installing many new PV systems. These systems may be unsafe (not code-compliant) at initial installation, may develop hazardous conditions over the life of the system, may be hazardous to operate or service, and may fail to deliver the full performance of a well-designed and installed PV system.

The authority having jurisdiction (AHJ) is the key player in ensuring that these less-than-good PV installations do not proliferate further. Inspectors need to demand additional training in the inspection of PV systems and then inspect these systems very closely. Yes, it is a relatively unfamiliar technology, but 80% of the *Code* already familiar to inspectors applies, and it is relatively easy to learn the inspection requirements that are unique to PV systems.

Several organizations are providing training and certification for individuals in the PV industry. The training, experience, and skill requirements of PV designers/installers obtaining this certification will help to ensure that safer, higher quality PV systems are installed.

PV System Types

Two main types of PV systems are being installed in the U.S.: utility-interactive (grid-connected) (photo 2-1) and stand-alone (off grid) (photo 2-2). Both

PHOTO 2.1 200 kW carport PV system

types (photos 2-1, 2-2, 2-3 and 2-4) use PV modules connected in series and in parallel to form PV arrays that produce dc energy at various voltages from about 12 volts to 600 volts. See Article 100 and Section 690.2 of the *NEC* for definitions of the terms used to describe PV equipment and systems. Generally, energy storage batteries are found in the stand-alone systems but are not normally found in the utility-interactive systems. Variations of each system are possible with some utility-interactive systems having battery banks to provide energy when the utility power is not available. The larger residential stand-alone systems will usually have a back-up generator, and these systems are known as hybrid stand-alone systems.

Utility-Interactive Systems

Utility-Interactive (U-I) PV systems are by far the most numerous of the types of PV systems being installed. A typical residential system might have a PV array and an inverter (converts dc to ac) capable of delivering 2500–5000 watts of ac power to either ac loads in the house or to the utility grid when the PV power output is in excess of those local loads. In residential PV systems, single and multiple inverter installations are common. The single inverter may have an ac output rating of 700 to 7000 watts, and systems are frequently seen with 2–4 inverters used to increase the system power output (photo 2-7). A few residential PV systems have had ac outputs up to 90 kW!

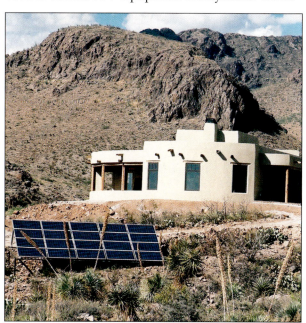

PHOTO 2.2 3.3 kW off-grid PV system

Chapter 2 — An Overview of PV Systems

PHOTO 2.3 6 kW utility-interactive inverter

These residential-sized inverters interface with the grid at 120 volts or 240 volts, are certified/listed to Underwriters Laboratories Standard for Safety 1741 (UL 1741) (inverters, combiners, and charge controllers), and have all of the necessary safety equipment built-in and verified as part of the listing process.

In commercial systems, the three-phase inverters commonly used usually start at about 10 kW, go up to 250 kW and to 1 MW (yes, 1 megawatt in a single inverter), and interface with the grid at 208–480 volts and higher (photo 2-8).

Stand-Alone Systems

Stand-alone systems are typically installed in remote areas where the utility grid is not available or where the connection fees to the grid are higher than the costs of an alternative energy system. While stand-alone systems sales are far smaller than the fast-growing utility-interactive PV system business, there is and has been a steady market for off-grid systems.

The stand-alone inverter converts dc energy stored in batteries by the PV array to ac energy to support the loads (photo 2-9). Inverter power ratings are from about 250 watts to 6000 watts for residential systems and, as before, multiple inverters may be connected together for greater power outputs. Battery banks usually operate at a nominal 12, 24, or 48 volts so the current levels to the inverters can be hundreds of amps at full load.

Larger stand-alone systems are found at na-

PHOTO 2.4 5 kW utility-interactive PV array. Electricity and shade.

PHOTO 2.5 250 kW utility-interactive inverter

PHOTO 2.6 Inverters and charge controllers for 10 kW off-grid/stand-alone PV system

PHOTO 2.9 Two 5 kW stand-alone inverters

PHOTO 2.7 Two utility-interactive inverters for more power

PHOTO 2.10 Framed PV modules (anodized aluminum or brown)

PHOTO 2.8 100 kW utility-interactive inverter

PHOTO 2.11 PV modules as roofing material

Chapter 2 — An Overview of PV Systems

Looking forward to 2014

New definitions were added to the code to address the actual functioning of equipment that is being installed.

DC-to-DC converters are now defined in 690.2 and they are the devices that are used between the output of the individual PV modules and the "string" inverters (higher voltage inverters operating at above 125 VDC). They are intended to segregate the operation of each PV module in the PV array from the operation of other modules in the PV array with the intent to reduce the effects of shading on the entire array. These listed devices vary considerably in configuration, operation and installation requirements and the code does not (and could not) deal specifically with each and every separate device. The instruction manual provided with these listed devices and the labels on the listed devices must be followed in order to ensure that they are installed in a code-compliant manner (110.3 B).

These dc-to-dc converters isolate the output of the PV module from the string circuit and the outputs of other PV modules. With this electronic isolation, the standard procedures for calculating maximum system voltage, short-circuit current, and other operating parameters of the module cannot be used when evaluating the output of the dc-to-dc converter.

Direct-current (dc) combiners are now defined in the *Code* and cover all devices that actually are used in the combining of direct currents in the PV dc circuits. A proliferation of names was being used including "source circuit" combiners, "recombiners", "output circuit" combiners and the like. The single term *dc combiner* can be used with additional modifiers to indicate any type of combiner.

A definition of *multimode inverter* was added to indicate that such devices are being used in utility interactive systems with battery backup capabilities. When the utility is present, the multimode inverter, typically keeps the connected batteries fully charged, and provides utility interactive power flow to and from the utility. When the utility is not present, the multimode inverter acts as a stand-alone inverter and provides designated load circuits with power from the batteries and/or the PV array. The listing on these multimode inverters and the separate utility-interactive ac input/output and standalone output circuits keep the system safe in all operating modes. Both the utility interactive and stand-alone sections of the code will apply to these multimode inverters.

Although not addressed by the 2014 *Code*, certain utility interactive inverters will be on the market that have special controls on the output that will allow power factor control and output voltage variations outside of the limits established by UL Standard 1741. The standard is being modified to address these new inverters. These extra variations in the output parameters can be used only when permitted by the utility.

tional parks, telecomm sites, and federal facilities. These can be as small as the residential system with ac outputs in the 2–10 kW range, but they can also have single inverters up to 250 kW. A few of these larger systems have multiple large inverters with combined outputs approaching 500 kW or more. Battery banks for the larger systems operate in the 200–600 volt range and dc currents to the inverters can be hundreds of amps at these higher voltages.

Component Descriptions

PV Modules

The first thing the inspector sees are the PV modules. While most of them have glass fronts, aluminum frames (colored mill-finish aluminum or anodized brown or black (photo 2-10) and plastic backs, some will be made with plastic frames or with no frames. Others will be used as roofing materials (photo 2-11) or laminated directly to standing seam metal roofs (photo 2-12). PV modules come in many sizes and shapes. The inspector needs to determine the listing of the modules and the electrical ratings. These are usually printed on the back of the module or are available in the instruction manual. Some unlisted, custom modules are being installed in architect-designed projects, and unlisted modules no longer meet *Code*

PHOTO 2.12 Thin film PV modules laminated to a metal standing seam roof

requirements [690.4(D)]. Although appearances may differ, these PV modules all produce electricity when illuminated, and the normal cautions associated with any electrical power system should be followed. PV modules come in differing power and voltage ratings and the sizes and ratings are continually changing. The modules must be connected in a manner that produces the needed voltage, current, and power since the output of a single module is usually not sufficient.

PV Combiners

PV combiners (PV j-boxes or PV combining enclosures) are common in PV systems operating at dc nominal voltages of 12, 24, and 48 volts and are also used in higher voltage systems (up to 600 volts). They must be certified/listed by a nationally recognized testing laboratory (NRTL) to UL Standard 1741 [690.4(D)]. In these systems, it is a normal practice to connect modules in series [called a PV source circuit (690.2)] to get the proper voltage and then to connect each series source circuits of modules in parallel with other source circuits through a PV combiner to increase the current to get the desired power level. These combiners will usually contain the overcurrent devices (fuses in the high voltage systems or circuit breakers in the 12-, 24-, 48-volt systems) that are required to protect the module interconnecting conductors from fault currents and the individual modules from reverse currents. The reverse currents may originate from parallel-connected strings of modules, from reverse currents from the batteries in a system that has them, or from backfeed currents from a utility-interactive inverter (unlikely in listed inverters).

The ratings of the overcurrent devices in the combiners must be consistent with the ampacity of the conductors connecting the modules in the source circuit and less than the rating of maximum series fuse marked on the back of the module. The combiner might be viewed as a branch-circuit load center connected in reverse acting like a PV source-circuit combining panel. The overcurrent devices in this enclosure are located in the proper place in the PV circuits to meet *NEC* and UL requirements. Many of these enclosures are white since they may be exposed to sunlight and white minimizes the internal temperature rise (photos 2-13 and 2-14). Note that the combiner in photo 2-13 has black-colored conductors instead of the white insulation required

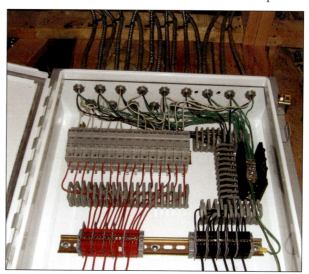

PHOTO 2.13 PV combiner with incorrect color codes. Black conductors should have white insulation.

PHOTO 2.14 PV combiner in white enclosure with circuit breakers. Note exposed busbars, but code-compliant with screw down cover.

Chapter 2 — An Overview of PV Systems

PHOTO 2.15 50-A charge controller with remote display
Courtesy of Blue Sky Energy

PHOTO 2.16 60-A charge controller

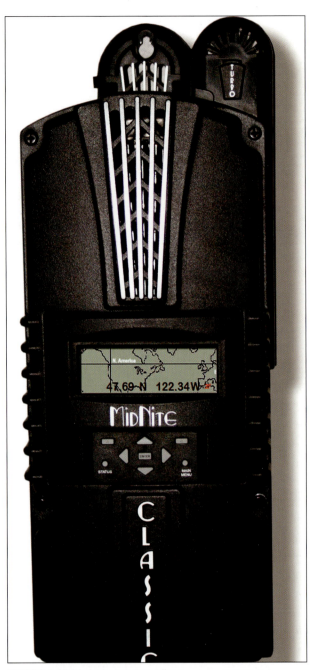

PHOTO 2.17 96-A charge controller *Courtesy of MidNite Solar*

Charge Controllers

Stand-alone systems and utility-interactive (U-I) systems with battery banks will also have charge controllers that regulate the state-of-charge of the battery bank. Charge controllers come in many sizes, shapes, and colors (photos 2-15, 2-16 and 2-17). When properly adjusted, they protect the batteries from being overcharged. The installer is responsible for adjusting these devices properly. Inspectors should verify good field terminations, proper conductor sizes, and appropriate overcurrent devices protecting those conductors.

by the *Code* for grounded conductors. Inspectors should check for screw-cover enclosures and warning labels if the combiner contains circuit breakers or fuses and also has internal, exposed, energized terminals. UL Standard 1741 may be changed to reflect the requirement for such warning labels and in the future may require the combiners to be deadfront when opened. Some combiners are presently deadfront.

PHOTO 2.18 Dual 4 kW utility-interactive inverters

Inverters

Inverters are found in both stand-alone systems and U-I systems. They essentially convert direct current (dc) energy from the PV system (and the dc energy stored in batteries) to alternating current (ac) energy for use by local loads or for feeding into the utility system (photos 2-18, 2-19, and 2-20). Some U-I inverters, known as multi-mode inverters, have the capability to power standby load circuits from batteries when the utility is down.

Many PV owners in California were surprised when their utility-interactive PV systems did not work during the energy-shortage-created rolling utility blackouts and brownouts a few years ago. Utility-interactive PV systems with multi-mode inverters and battery backup were popular for months following the blackouts.

Unfortunately, installation manuals for these complex inverters (particularly the stand-alone types) can be several hundred pages long. The inspector should verify the proper dc and ac conductor sizes and overcurrent protection. *See* Appendix D. Both are based on the rated ac power output of the inverter. *See* Sections 690.8 and 690.9 in the *NEC Handbook*.

The utility-interactive inverters have all of the automatic ac utility disconnect devices built-in that protect the utility linemen who are working on a supposedly unenergized utility feeder. The utility-interactive PV inverter will not energize a

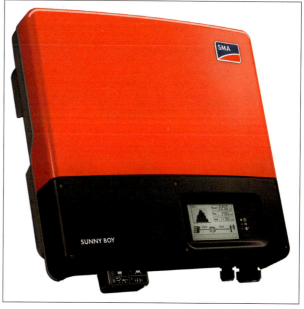

PHOTO 2.19 Transformerless Inverter *Courtesy SMA Technologies AG*

dead line and in fact will disconnect from the line when the line voltage varies more than -12% to +10% from nominal (typically 120, 208, 240, 277, or 480 volts) or when the frequency varies by more than -0.7 to +0.5 Hertz from the normal 60 Hz. The inverter monitors the utility line voltage and frequency, and that voltage and frequency must remain stable and within tolerance for five minutes before the inverter can resume power transfer from the dc output of the PV system to the ac loads or to the utility.

Chapter 2 — An Overview of PV Systems

PHOTO 2.20 Multimode Inverter *Courtesy SMA Technologies AG*

PHOTO 2.21 DC ground-fault detection device by Outback Power.

All PV systems, with rare exceptions, must have an anti-fire device known as a ground-fault detection/interruption device (GFID). *See* 690.5. These GFIDs are normally built into all utility-interactive inverters as a fuse that blows on ground faults. The stand-alone inverter will usually not include the Section 690.5 ground-fault device, so if it is not built into the charge controller, an external, field-installed ground-fault protective device must be used. Photo 2-21 shows a typical GFID used on off-grid PV systems. The author developed this system of circuit breakers in 1990.

PV Electrical Characteristics

PV modules generate voltage and current when exposed to sunlight, either direct or indirect (dusk or dawn). To get a better understanding of the photovoltaic effect and how it produces electricity from sunlight, it is suggested that a good physics book be consulted

These modules are current-limited current sources unlike voltage sources such as the common 120-V ac receptacle outlet or the output of a gasoline-fired generator or a battery. The magnitude of the current output and the power output is directly related to the intensity of the sunlight; the brighter the sunlight, the more current the PV module can deliver. The maximum current is related to the size of the module and the size of the cells it contains. The voltage output varies as the load on the PV module is changed and is an inverse function of temperature. The output voltage increases as the temperature decreases. Utility-interactive inverters and some charge controllers vary the load on the PV array to extract maximum power from the PV array under varying conditions of sunlight intensity and temperature. More on these concepts will be discussed in chapter 3.

With the PV power, dc current, and voltage varying with both sunlight and temperature (even to the extent of exceeding the specified rated output of the system), it becomes evident that designing the electrical system to allow for these variations or to develop code requirements may not be a simple task. In all cases, the PV system will consist of separate components that must be connected during the installation according to the requirements of the *National Electrical Code*. The plan reviewers and inspectors are responsible for ensuring that those *NEC* requirements are met.

INSPECTORS and PLAN REVIEWERS Homework:

Download sales brochures from the Internet from PV sales/installation organizations, inverter manufacturers, and module manufacturers.

Visit the author's website to read past *IAEI News* "Perspectives on PV" articles.

Join IAEI to keep abreast of the latest developments in the *IAEI News*.

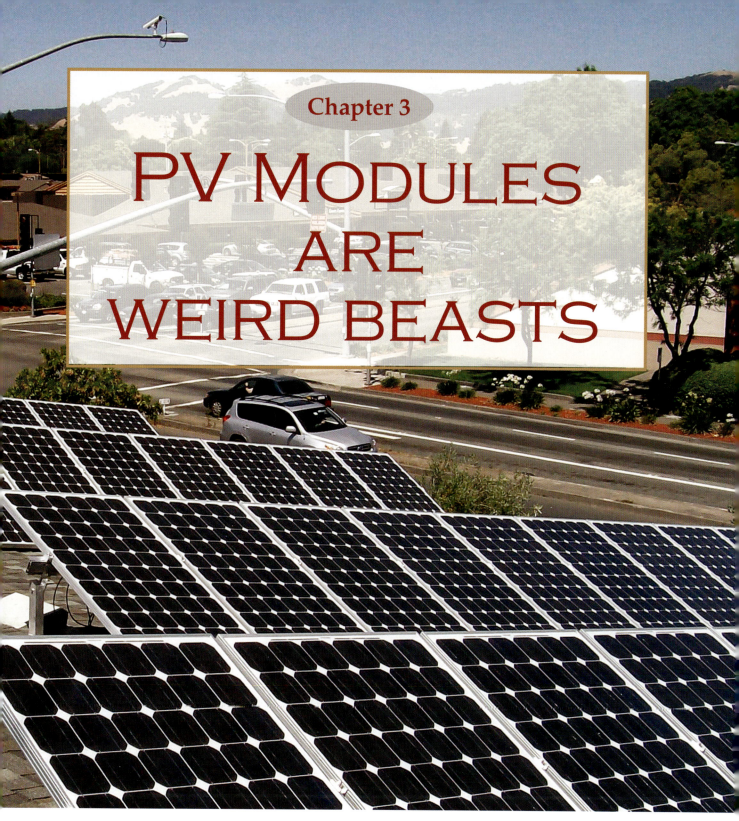

Chapter 3
PV Modules Are Weird Beasts

In order to understand how and why the *Code* is different for PV systems compared to other electrical systems, we must first delve into the mysteries of what they are and how they operate. Inspectors need to be familiar with these unique characteristics of PV modules because the ampacity calculations and overcurrent device ratings don't follow the usual rules of thumb being used in the electrical trades. Additionally, many PV installers are not using the proper calculations either.

Current Sources

PV modules are current sources of energy, as opposed to voltage sources like the 120-volt ac outlet in the home or office or the 12-volt dc battery in the car. The output of a PV module, in terms of voltage and current, depends on the load placed on that module. The output is direct current (dc), and the load is typically supplied by a utility-interactive inverter, which changes the dc energy into alternating current (ac) energy.

Standard Test Conditions

PV modules are rated for voltage and current output when exposed to a set of standard test conditions. The standard solar intensity (called *irradiance*) is set at 1000 watts per square meter (W/m^2). This is an international constant and is near the average value of irradiance at sea level on the surface of the earth. Modules are also rated at a standard module/cell temperature of 25 degrees Celsius (C) [77 degrees Fahrenheit (F)]. These two values of irradiance and temperature are referred to as *standard test conditions* (STC). When the module is exposed to these standard test conditions, and connected to the correct load, the module will produce the rated power at a maximum power point voltage (V_{mp}) and with a maximum power point current (I_{mp}).

During the evaluation of the safety to the module [performed by a nationally recognized testing laboratory (NRTL)] leading to the module being listed as required by *NEC* 690.4(D), the ratings of the module are also verified to be within some percentage of the label values. The tolerance on the label values is usually 10 percent but may be as low as 3 percent.

A PV module can be short-circuited indefinitely without damage. And, as we will see in later chapters, the wiring, the switchgear and the overcurrent protection are designed in a way that will allow entire PV arrays to be short-circuited without damage.

Current and Voltage Measurements — The IV Curve

Measuring the module or array output under short circuit conditions will allow us to obtain a measurement of the short-circuit current (I_{sc}), which will be used in PV system sizing and in many *Code* calculations. A voltage measurement under short-circuit conditions will yield zero (0) volts.

If a voltmeter is used to measure the voltage output of a PV module or array that is not connected to any load, the voltage obtained will be the open-circuit (no load) voltage (V_{oc}). A current measurement would be zero (0) for this open-circuit condition.

If simultaneous voltage and current measurements are taken on a PV module or a PV array and these measurements plotted for various loads, a graph that shows the electrical characteristics of a PV module could be shown. The graph would have current (I) on the vertical axis and voltage (V) on the horizontal axis. This graph or plot is shown in figure 3-1 and is called an IV curve.

The point to the right on the horizontal axis is the open circuit-voltage (V_{oc}) and the current at this point is zero (0). On the vertical current axis, the curve intersects the axis at the short-circuit current (I_{sc}) where the voltage is zero.

Power Equals Voltage Multiplied by Current

Each point on the IV curve represents a value of voltage and a value of current at a particular load. Multiplying the voltage (V) by the current (I) will calculate the power (P) produced by a module and delivered to the load.

$P = V \times I$

From this relationship, it can be seen that the module delivers no power at either the open-circuit voltage point or at the short-circuit current point because one of the factors of power is zero at these points.

However, if we look at the other points on the curve (producing power from different loads), we can see that the power is not zero for these points. If the power output curve is added to the IV curve, we get the graph shown in figure 3-2 that includes the IV curve in blue and the power curve in red. The horizontal axis for the combined graph is still volts, but the vertical axis (on the right) for the power curve is now marked watts. The curve for power shows that it reaches a peak for some load between I_{sc} and V_{oc} and this point is called the maximum power point (P_{mp}). Associated with the maximum power point are a maximum power point voltage (V_{mp}) and a maximum power point current (I_{mp}).

It should be noted that the output voltage of a PV module is not constant and varies with the load. And this output is changed by several different ex-

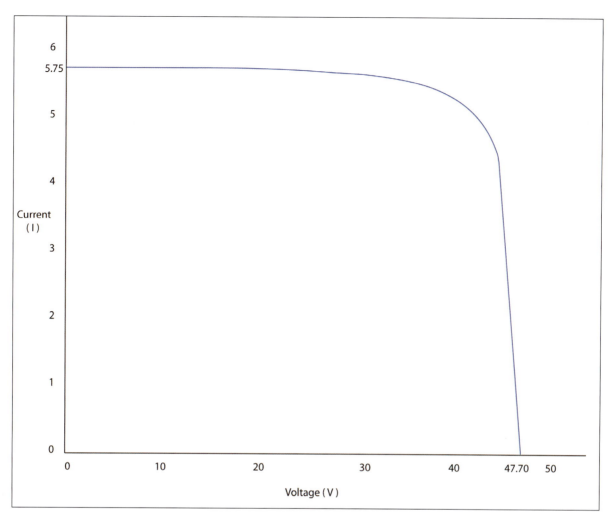

FIGURE 3.1 IV Curve for a PV module

ternal environmental conditions in addition to the connected load.

Sunlight Produces Current

The current output of a PV module is directly proportional to the intensity of the sunlight falling on it. The rated currents (both I_{sc} and I_{mp}) are output at the standard test condition irradiance of 1000 W/m². However, PV modules are exposed to irradiance values from 0 (night) to 1500 W/m² (cloud, water, snow, or sand enhanced) and the current follows changes in the intensity of the sunlight. A 10% reduction in the irradiance value will result in a 10% reduction in I_{sc} and I_{mp}. However, the open circuit voltage (V_{oc}) is relatively unchanged with variations in irradiance. Figure 3-3 shows the IV curves for a PV module as the sunlight intensity varies from 1000 W/m² down to 500 W/m². As can be seen, the I_{sc} changes in direct proportion to changes in irradiance but V_{oc} and V_{mp} do not vary nearly as much.

This is a significant fact. The voltage on a PV module or PV array will generally be present at very low levels of light such as at dawn or dusk. PV arrays can have hundreds of volts on the wiring at dawn and dusk even before the sun directly illuminates the front of the modules. Hazardous voltages on exposed terminals will be present.

A second variation in the module output and the IV curve is caused by temperature. Module current is relatively insensitive to temperature, but both the V_{oc} and V_{mp} voltages will be affected. In crystalline PV modules, V_{oc} varies inversely with temperature at about 0.5%/degree Celsius and peak-power voltage (V_{mp}) varies inversely about 0.4% per degree Celsius. Figure 3-4 shows the relationship and it can be seen that as temperature goes down, voltage increases.

Turn Off the Light

The PV modules in utility-interactive systems are connected in series and the open-circuit voltage

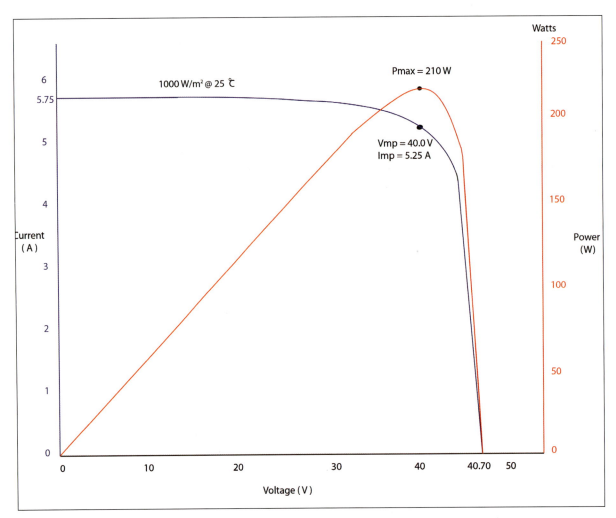

FIGURE 3.2 IV and Power Curve

may approach 600 volts in cold weather. The only way to effectively turn off all electricity from a PV module or a PV array is to cover it with an opaque material. Working at night on the array wiring is an option, but worker safety would be a concern, and lighting illuminating the distant sky has been known to illuminate the array enough to produce electric shocks.

Determining the PV Size and Output to Match the Inverter

In the PV design process, the array output must be matched to the utility-interactive inverter input. As noted previously, the module voltage and current outputs are not constant and the system designer must first ensure that in cold weather conditions, the array output voltage will not exceed the voltage rating of the inverter, the conductor insulation, or other connected equipment. This limit will frequently be as high as 600 volts. In a similar manner, all conductors, overcurrent devices, and switchgear must be able to handle the array output current under worst-case conditions of high sunlight intensity. Exceeding the voltage rating on inverters, conductors, switchgear or other equipment would be a code violation and has been known to damage such equipment. See *NEC* 110.3(B).

Early pioneers in PV including PV module manufacturers, Jet Propulsion Laboratories (space programs), Underwriters Laboratories (UL), and the National Fire Protection Association (NFPA) realized that because of these variations in the output of the PV module, special consideration would need to be made to handle these systems in the *National Electrical Code (NEC)*.

UL Standard 1703, *Flat-Plate Photovoltaic Modules and Panels*, was written to establish the safety requirements (mechanical and electrical) that PV modules would be required to meet. In the standard, up to about 2012, requirements in module instruction manuals were written that modified

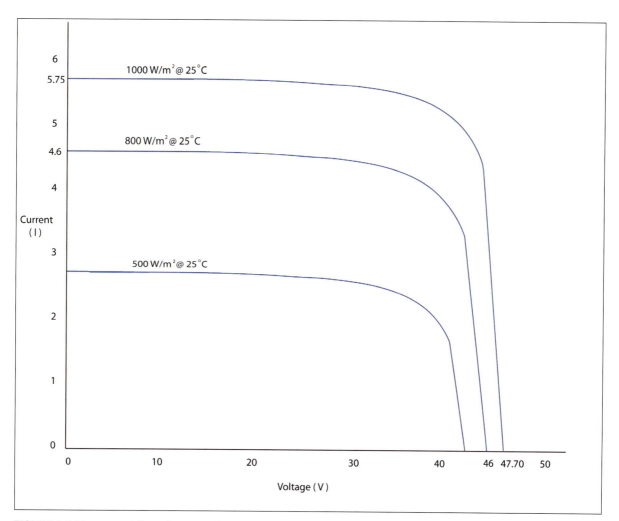

FIGURE 3.3 IV curve variations due to varying sunlight

the values of the standard test condition parameters printed on the back of the module. These modifications dealt with the fact that the sunlight intensity in many parts of the country could exceed the standard test condition of 1000W/m² for three hours of more on numerous days throughout the year. Yes, the PV module can deliver more than rated current and rated voltage as environmental conditions vary.

Three hours per day represents continuous duty in the *Code* and it was decided in the early days of PV systems that the code calculations for PV systems should be based on worst possible outputs and that those outputs would be considered to be continuous 24 hours per day / 7 days per week / 52 weeks per year and not vary on a daily cycle with the sun. Therefore all voltages and currents used in the calculations for PV systems in *Code* are adjusted from the standard test conditions measurements in a way that ensures that the electrical system will meet *Code* requirements for safety and that all of the equipment will be operated within limits established by both the *Code* and UL standards.

Adjustments — Short-Circuit Current

The first adjustment is made to the module short-circuit current. UL Standard 1703 required (until May 2012) that the module manufacturer have the following statement, or its equivalent, in the instruction manual that is shipped with every PV module.

"Multiply the short circuit current (I_{sc}) marked on the back of the module by 125% before applying any requirements established by the *NEC*."

This 125% factor is applied to the short-circuit current to ensure that the current used in any *Code* ampacity or overcurrent device rating calculations will never be exceeded by the actual module output under high irradiance conditions. A 125% factor on I_{sc} would be equivalent to expos-

Chapter 3 — PV Modules Are Weird Beasts

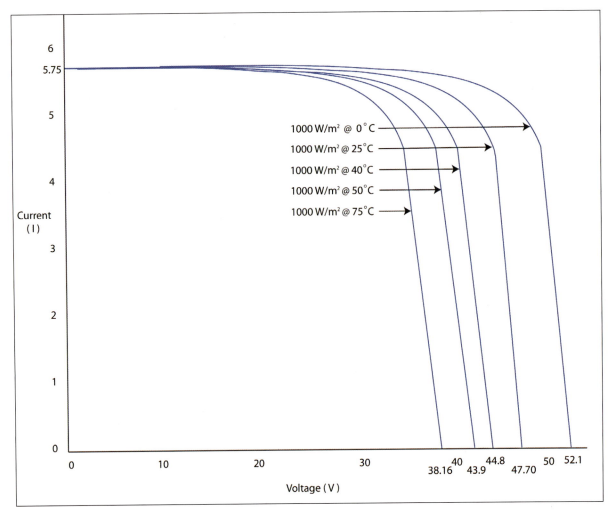

FIGURE 3.4 IV curve variations due to varying temperature

ing the module to 1250 W/m² of irradiance and that value of solar intensity has never been measured on a continuous basis.

Transient values of sunlight may reach 1500 W/m² due to cloud reflectivity enhancements and reflections off sand, water, and snow, but these conditions are short-term in nature since the clouds move, as does the sun (earth rotation). They are not stable situations and last for only a few minutes.

The instructions for most flat-plate PV modules prohibit the installation of any permanent light reflecting or light concentrating surface near the modules.

Adjustments — Open Circuit Voltage

As noted previously, the open-circuit voltage (V_{oc}) varies inversely with temperature. The instruction manuals for PV modules have the following statement or its equivalent:

"Multiply the open-circuit voltage (V_{oc}) marked on the back of the module by 125% before applying any requirements established by the *NEC*."

For crystalline silicon, a factor of 125% on V_{oc} represents the open-circuit voltage of a module at -40°C (-40°F). Temperatures lower than -40° are found in some parts of the country and further adjustments to V_{oc} may have to be made where these temperatures are expected.

NEC Leads UL Standard 1703

In 1996, during preparations for the *1999 NEC*, the PV Industry, UL, and NFPA reached a joint agreement to place all module output correction factors in the *Code*. Those proposals were agreed to by all, and the *1999 NEC* was modified accordingly.

In Section 690.8, a requirement was established to multiply the module short-circuit current by 125%. This *duplicated* the module manual instruction to adjust the I_{sc} to account for normal and expected irradiance values above 1000 W/m².

Since many areas of the country never have temperatures as low as -40°, a temperature-dependent table was added to Section 690.7 showing multiplication factors for V_{oc} that vary from 1.00 at an expected low temperature of 25°C (77°F) to 1.25 at -40°. Again, instructions in the module manual duplicated these *Code* requirements.

Since newer module technologies have different temperature coefficients than crystalline silicon, the *2008 NEC* requires that the module manufacturer's temperature coefficients be used where available rather than Table 690.7. See Appendix A on how to calculate module voltages using temperature coefficients.

UL has modified UL 1703 Standard in May 2012 to remove the 125% multipliers on V_{oc} and I_{sc} from the PV module instruction manuals. This solves a significant problem for inspectors and installers who are required to follow *NEC* section 110.3(B), which requires that all instructions with a listed product be followed. If followed, this section of the *Code* and 690.8 and 690.7 create a double calculation with far too conservative results. The module instruction manuals soon will be modified to remove these two requirements and only the *Code* requirements will remain. Pressures from electrical inspectors throughout the country were responsible for the changes.

A Second 125 Percent

Throughout the *NEC*, feeders and branch circuits, as well as overcurrent devices, are rated to operate on a continuous basis at no more than 80% of rating. Section 215.2(A)(1) has this phrase, also found in other sections of the *Code*:

"The minimum feeder circuit size, before the application of any adjustment or correction factors, shall have an allowable ampacity not less than the non-continuous load plus 125 percent of the continuous load."

The intent of this code requirement, other than the obvious rating factors, is that the 125 percent factor is not to be applied at the same time the "conditions of use" factors (temperature and conduit fill corrections on ampacity) are applied. From a math point of view 1.25 (125%) and 0.8 are reciprocals, so we can use them two ways. We can calculate the conductor size by taking 1.25 times the continuous load (continuous *current* for a PV or other genera-

Looking forward to 2014

Sections 690.7 and 690.8 were revised to allow PV system with maximum systems voltage to 1000 volts on installations other than one and two family dwellings. PV systems over 1000 volts are referred to Article 690, Part IX.

Sections 210.19(A)(1) Branch Circuits and 215.2(A)(1) Feeders have been modified to show ampacity calculations very much like those in 690.8(B). The conductor ampacity is based on the larger of 125% of the maximum current or on the maximum current after the corrections for conditions of use have been applied.

Most of the circuit identification, routing and installation requirements in 690.4 were moved to 690.31.

In circuits where the source of the power or energy for that circuit is a current-limited source such as a PV module, string of PV modules or utility interactive inverter, it is not possible for that source to provide currents that can damage the circuit. This is because the circuits are sized at least 125% of the maximum limited current from the source. These circuits can, however, be damaged from external sources of current from parallel connected PV source circuits or on the AC side, from back feed from the utility into faults in the circuit.

The location requirement for overcurrent devices established in section 240.21 of the code does not address these current-limited circuits. This section requires that the circuit be protected by an overcurrent device at the supply for the circuit.

Section 690.9 (A) now requires that these current limited circuits be protected from overcurrents at the source of those higher currents. This is why fuses are used at the ends of strings of modules in dc combiners and not at each individual module. And why circuit breakers are located in panelboards at the end of the inverter output circuits, and not near the inverter end of the circuit. In both cases, the source of currents that can damage the circuit is external to the circuit and is not the main source in the circuit.

PHOTO 3.1 PV DC Combiner

tor) or by taking 0.8 times the conductor ampacity (before adjustments for conditions of use) to see the maximum continuous currents.

This same 125 percent factor (or the conditons of use factors if they result in requiring a larger conductor) is applied to PV source and output circuits, so, in fact, we might multiply the short-circuit current by 1.25 twice before selecting a conductor or overcurrent device. A factor of 1.56 (1.25 x 1.25 = 1.56) is commonly used to determine ampacity but this is a short cut and the slightly more complex actual calculations will be addressed in Appendix D.

Unfortunately, the 125 percent multiplier on I_{sc} still remaining in the module instruction manuals on V_{oc} and I_{sc} continues to confuse many. PV designers, installers and inspectors should multiply I_{sc} by only two factors of 1.25, not three. V_{oc} should be calculated following the requirements of 690.7 and the factors will be less than 125% unless very low (-40°) temperatures are expected at the installation location.

Energized and Safe for Decades

We have seen how the module output varies with the environmental conditions. The *Code*-required corrections to the rated output are used to ensure that the system electrical equipment never has to handle more current or voltage than it was designed for. We have taken that rated output, adjusted it for worst-case conditions and then made the assumption that these worst-case conditions exist continually, even when we know the output goes to zero every night. PV modules will produce dangerous amounts of voltage and current for 40 years or more. These adjustments and the other *Code* requirements represent minimums to ensure that this sunlight-generated electricity is safely contained for that period of time and longer.

INSPECTORS and PLAN REVIEWERS

PLAN REVIEWERS:

Verify proper conductor types and ampacity calculations based on high average ambient temperatures.

Verify maximum dc PV system output voltage is less than the voltage rating of conductors, switchgear, overcurrent devices, inverters and other equipment.

INSPECTORS:

Verify that installed conductor types and sizes agree with plans.

Verify that the module and inverter types match the plans.

BOTH:

The next time you are vacuum cleaning at home, note the 12-amp number on the front of the vacuum cleaner. Taking 125% of this value turns out to be the 15-amp rating on a typical branch circuit. The *NEC* and UL Standards are at work protecting you and yours.

Photovoltaic Power Systems

> Proper grounding will always be a code requirement.

Chapter 4

Connecting the Module to Mother Earth

When buying real estate, conventional wisdom dictates the three most important elements are location, location, and location. The author, based on twenty-eight years of working with PV systems, including the school of hard knocks, strongly feels that the three most important elements to short- and long-term PV safety are Grounding, Grounding, and Grounding.

Grounding is important and will be covered not only in this chapter, but also throughout subsequent chapters. In this chapter, we are starting with the equipment grounding of metal-framed PV modules.

Because most PV modules are made with aluminum frames, these exposed metal conductive surfaces must be grounded (250.110). Aluminum is a difficult metal to ground because it has an oxidized surface that is an electrical insulator. Furthermore, PV module manufacturers frequently anodize the surface for different colors and also clear coat the surface. Both of these surface treatments are also insulators that can make electrical grounding of the module difficult, while at the same time not preventing electrical shocks when touching a faulted module.

Utility-interactive residential (dwelling unit), commercial, and megawatt PV systems operate with dc voltages from 50 volts to 600 volts and higher. AC voltages start at 120 and go to 23 kV on some of the larger systems. Underwriters Laboratories (UL) has determined that there is a shock hazard in exposed circuits operating at over 30 volts (ac or dc) in wet locations. See *NEC* 690.31(A) and 690.33(C).

Operating currents range from less than 10 amps dc and ac to about 2200 amps dc on some of the larger inverters. An arc at currents around 1 amp can start a fire in the right material. Module power can be as low as 20 watts, but ranges upward to 320 watts. Consider the small 7-watt night-light or Christmas tree bulb (before LEDs). Seven watts can start a fire.

PV modules and wiring as well as outdoor-mounted inverters are subjected to severe environmental conditions. Rain, sleet, snow, hail, sand, wind, and sunlight coupled with low and high temperatures would wear down the most stalwart postal worker over a 40–50 year span — the life expectancy of a PV module for producing dangerous amounts of voltage and current. USE-2 cables and the new PV Cables are some of the toughest generally available cables and we have seen USE-2 holding up well after 25 years when properly installed. But what about a less-than-outstanding installation after 10 or 20 years?

The environmental conditions, the use of copper conductors to ground aluminum module frames, and the daily thermal cycling that terminals, combiners, and modules are subjected to will eventually cause a breakdown in the insulations involved or in the electrical connections. A breakdown of insulation or the failure of electrical connections can result in nearby conductive surfaces being energized and posing both shock and fire hazards.

Proper grounding is a must, even when the *NEC* and the UL Standards do not fully address the issue.

PHOTO 4.1 Improper module grounding: Plated steel thread cutting screw not corrosion-resistant, THHN conductors and nylon lug not UV-rated

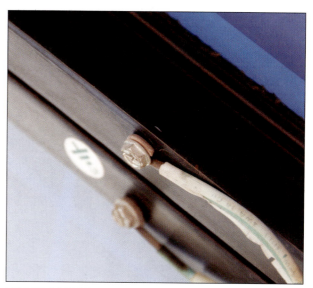

PHOTO 4.3 THHN conductor, thread cutting screw and copper in contact with aluminum

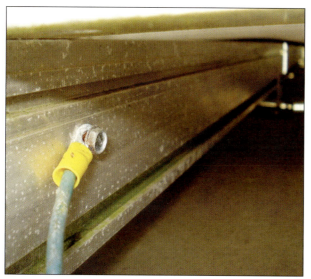

PHOTO 4.2 Improper lugs and conductors, not securely fastened

Module Grounding Problems Are Being Observed and Reported

Tens of thousands of PV systems are being installed annually with financial incentives available at the federal and state levels (http://www.dsireusa.org/). Payments for net energy generated and for all energy produced from renewable sources are being made by utility companies in some states and these payments are also contributing to increasing numbers of PV installations.

Unfortunately, getting the PV modules and racks grounded in a manner that will yield a low resistance connection to the grounding system for 50 or more years appears to be difficult. Inspectors are seeing improper grounding techniques being used (photos 4-1, 4-2, and 4-3). Improper grounding instructions are even appearing in the instruction manuals for listed PV modules (photo 4-4). Inspections and tests of installed PV systems have found that in some cases, module-grounding connections have deteriorated in as little as three years and sooner in some areas (photos 4-5 and 4-6).

Significant confusion exists among module manufacturers, PV installers, and the inspectors concerning how to properly ground a PV module, and that confusion is becoming more and more apparent as numerous PV systems are being installed. A little history may highlight the cause of this confusion.

A Look at UL Standard 1703

The current edition (2012) of Underwriters Laboratories (UL) Standard 1703, *PV Flat Plate Modules and Panels*, delineates the differences between *grounding* and *bonding*. Bonding refers to the factory-made electrical connections between the four or more aluminum sections of the module frame. Grounding refers to the field-installed electrical connection between the aluminum module frame and the equipment-grounding system (usually consisting of copper conductors).

Bonding the frame pieces together in the factory using very specific materials and methods results in a durable electrical connection between the frame pieces so that any failure in the module insulation or external conductor insulation will

PHOTO 4.4 Installed per instruction manual—but copper touching aluminum?

PHOTO 4.5 Improper use of module bonding screw and copper in braid touching aluminum

PHOTO 4.6 Tinned copper braid offers no protection for aluminum module frame.

result in all pieces of the frame receiving equal voltage. The factory bonding also insures that when the module frame is properly field-grounded at one of the marked and tested points, the entire module frame is maintained at the ground (earth) potential under fault conditions.

During the bonding process, all screw fasteners (when used) are precisely torqued to the specified value by automated equipment or by trained technicians using torque screwdrivers. The factory bonding materials and methods are evaluated for low resistance and durability during the certification/listing process. Subsequent to the listing, if the manufacturer changes any of the bonding materials or methods, the changes must be reevaluated by the listing agency. The materials (including any screws or washers) are not specified generically; they are specified to the original equipment manufacturers (OEM) and must always be obtained and used from those sources unless any change is reevaluated by the certification/listing agency.

Contrast this precisely controlled and evaluated factory bonding system with the field-installed grounding techniques used to connect a copper equipment-grounding conductor to the aluminum module frame. Grounding PV modules is haphazard at best for a number of reasons. The first is that the module manufacturers do not realize the importance of this connection to the overall safety of the system. The revised UL 1703 clearly distinguishes the differences between bonding and grounding. The manufacturers have the impression that the bonding techniques and materials used in the factory may be applied to the grounding connections made by the installer in the field. Instruction manuals and hardware (sometimes supplied) show techniques that are not consistent with good electrical connections (see photo 4-4). Field-made connections using a threaded fastener are rarely torqued to the specified value even when that value is given in the module instruction manual, because few PV installers have or carry torque screwdrivers or wrenches. The field grounding connections may or may not be inspected by the AHJ and they are never tested for overall continuity. Also, since the PV system can operate without trouble for many

PHOTO 4.7 One method of grounding a PV module when all else fails

years, there is little motivation to inspect these connections after the original installation.

In late 2007, UL issued an "Interpretation" of UL 1703 (included in UL 1703) which focused on module field grounding. This interpretation is also known as a Certification Requirement Decision (CRD). This interpretation was to be used by module manufacturers and the module testing/certification/listing laboratories (UL, CSA, TUV and ETL) to evaluate and possibly revise the grounding methods, hardware (if any) and instructions supplied with the modules. Unfortunately, it is not possible for the laboratories to review all existing modules and supposedly modules are reevaluated every five years when the listing must be renewed. A few module manufacturers have revised their grounding instructions, but it would appear that these revised instructions, in some cases, may have not been carefully evaluated or even reviewed by the certification/listing laboratories.

Grounding Instructions Not Consistent

For example, some instructions list lock washers, star washers and other critical grounding hardware that is distributed by major national hardware stores that maintain no source control over their suppliers. These common hardware products have not been evaluated as grounding devices or even as electrical equipment. These hardware products are not supplied by OEM vendors. Other PV module manufacturers continue to use or recommend thread cutting or thread forming screws when the UL Interpretation says that all threaded fasteners must be installed and removed ten times without damage to any threads. This requirement is nearly impossible to meet with the soft aluminum used for module frames.

The UL Interpretation of UL 1703 has very specific information about not putting dissimilar metals into contact and gives a chart that shows the

Looking forward to 2014

Module grounding continues to require close attention and inspection. The requirements of the revised (March 2012) Underwriters Laboratory Standard 1703 have not permeated throughout the entire module industry (including PV module manufacturers who write the module instruction manuals, and PV installers who install the modules). The instruction manuals for the PV module should completely describe the method(s) of grounding the module. The PV module manufacturer should not show grounding methods using commonly available hardware to make electrical connections because that hardware has not been evaluated for electrical properties nor has it been evaluated with the particular module.

A number of listed grounding devices are available that have been evaluated for grounding PV modules. However, unless the module manufacturer specifically mentions one or more of those grounding devices, and indicates that they have been evaluated with the module, then it is not possible to use those listed devices, because the coatings on modules vary significantly in thickness from module model to model and from manufacturer to manufacturer. Without specific tests, it is not possible to establish that the grounding device will penetrate the coatings and make a long lasting contact.

A revised section 690.47 (D) has been returned to the code after having been removed in the 2011 *Code*. The reference to section 250.54 indicates that this auxiliary array-grounding electrode does not have to be bonded to other grounding electrodes in the system. The requirement applies to ground-mounted arrays and roof-mounted arrays on dwellings. An existing grounding electrode may be used if the grounding electrode conductor falls to earth within 6 feet of the existing electrode. A grounding electrode conductor sized per 250.166 is required to ground the array frames or structure. In ground-mounted arrays, if the mounting structure meets the requirements for a grounding electrode, the structure may be used as the grounding electrode for the array. Also, if building steel is being used as a grounding electrode, the array structure may be grounded to building steel.

compatibility of various metals. Copper and aluminum may not come in contact and if they do, the aluminum at the contact point will be removed by galvanic corrosion destroying the connection. Inadvertent contact between the bare copper equipment-grounding conductor and an aluminum module frame or rack does not pose problems because the small amount of aluminum that may disappear is not involved in a required electrical contact.

In some cases, the instructions specify the use of a stainless-steel washer to isolate the copper conductor from the aluminum frame, but no surface preparation of the oxidized, anodized, and/or clear-coated aluminum module frame is specified. If this method were to be done properly with surface preparation, then the presumption is that the mechanical fastener (screw and nut) and the stainless steel washer would carry the fault currents. But these devices are generic in nature and have not been evaluated for carrying current.

A casual examination of any common electrical device such as a circuit breaker, a receptacle outlet, or a wall switch will show that the mechanical fastener provides only pressure to push the two electrical conductors together. Those mechanical fasteners (screws) are not normally designed or specified to carry currents, unless they have been specifically tested and evaluated to do so during the listing of the device. An example of a device where the provided screw has been evaluated to carry current is the neutral-to-ground bonding screw used in many service-entrance panels.

To further confuse the situation, it appears that the high currents, steel plates, and test methods used in UL Standard 467 for evaluating and listing grounding devices may not be applicable to evaluating grounding devices used to ground PV modules and racks where the currents are low and the aluminum surfaces are oxidized, anodized or clear coated.

Grounding the Array—690.47(D)

Section 690.47(D) in the *2008 NEC* is somewhat difficult to understand. The original proposal was to enter an optional PV array grounding method to reduce potential lightning damage. This optional module frame/array rack grounding method would have been installed along the lines of 250.54 and the new grounding electrode *would not* be required to be bonded to any other grounding electrodes. Unfortunately, the issue of bonding in section 250.54 was not addressed and array grounding is now mandatory. Exception 1 to this requirement appears to except the requirement when the array and the inverter or other loads are in the same structure such as a traffic warning sign. In high lightning areas, adding this new array grounding system might still be a good idea even when the inverter and the array are on the same building. Exception 2 says that if the existing grounding electrode can be reached with no more than a six-foot horizontal run, then it can be used instead of a new ground rod—lightning does not like to turn corners.

Help Has Arrived

The revisions to UL Standard 1703 discussed above are in place and module manufacturers and the testing, certification, and listing NRTLs are gradually applying these requirements to the modules. The UL Outline of Investigation 2703 is being harmonized with the module grounding requirements so that both the mounting racks and the modules may be properly grounded for the necessary decades.

One method used by utility companies for many years to connect copper conductors to aluminum busbars in an outdoor environment uses surface preparation and a tin-plated copper lay-in lug listed for direct burial. A description of this method is presented in Appendix C and is based on the instructions found in the Burndy Technical Section of their grounding devices catalog (see photo 4-7).

Summary

Grounding, both equipment and system, is critical to the short- and long-term public safety of PV systems. These systems may be producing power fifty years from the installation date with possibly deteriorating electrical connections and insulations. Grounding all exposed metal surfaces for the life of the systems is mandatory and the techniques used may have to exceed existing *Code* and UL requirements. Additional grounding requirements throughout the system will be covered in each chapter.

INSPECTORS and PLAN REVIEWERS

PLAN REVIEWERS:

Check that module grounding and other equipment grounding conductors are shown on the diagram.

Verify that a grounding detail is shown or is described in the module instruction manual submitted with the plans.

Verify that a separate array grounding system (in addition to the required equipment-grounding conductors) is shown on ground-mounted arrays and arrays on separate structures. (2008 *NEC*)

INSPECTORS:

Look for that PV connection to a new or existing grounding electrode.

After verifying that at least some part of the PV system has been connected to Earth, **inspect** all exposed metal surfaces to ensure proper grounding.

Insure that the modules are properly grounded. Surface preparation may be required to remove clear coats, anodizing or oxidation.

Verify that a dc grounding electrode conductor is properly routed from the inverter, charge controller or separate ground-fault protective device to a grounding electrode or to a grounding bar in load center.

Chapter 4 — Connecting the Module to Mother Earth

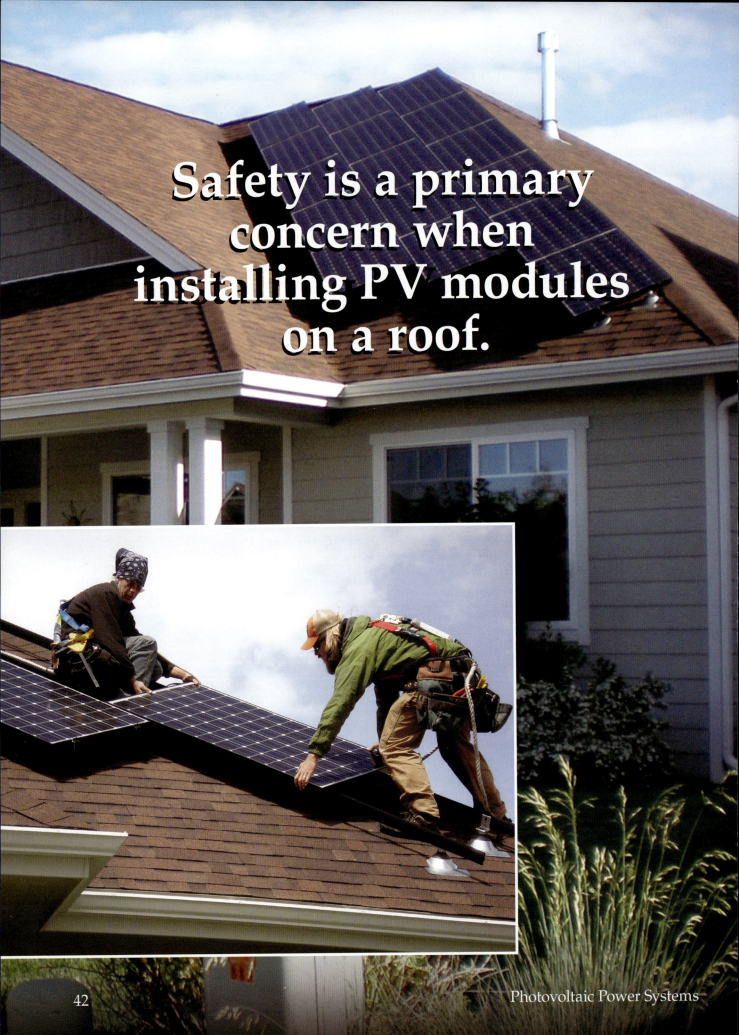

Chapter 5
PV Modules

Photovoltaic power systems can be examined in a number of different ways. In this book, we will start with the modules at the top of the system and progress through the system to the grid interconnection at the bottom. A utility-interactive PV system is a series-connected system, so where we start our examination is not important and if you are in a hurry for information on some part of the system that we have not gotten to, you can jump ahead to the chapter of interest.

The PV Array—Mechanical Considerations

The PV array consists of individual PV modules attached to a metal rack, and that rack is usually attached to the structural members of the roof in a typical rooftop-mounted residential utility-interactive PV system. Although not an electrical-code issue, some attention must be given to the attachment of the PV array to the building structure.

Most roofs in recent years have been built using span tables in the building codes or using trusses designed by professional engineers. PV arrays may add up to 4–5 pounds per square foot of dead weight to the roof structural members, and that weight will be concentrated through the rack mounting feet. Also, because the PV array is mounted above the roof some distance (zero to six inches or more), the roof may be subjected to both uplift and down-force wind loadings—again concentrated through the mounting feet of the rack. If the roof has several layers of old shingles under the array, the structural limit of the roof may be approached. Leaving as many as two layers of old shingles in place is a common practice during re-roofing, so we can assume that the basic roofing structure has a safety factor allowing the extra load of old shingles *or* the PV array, but possibly not several layers of shingles *and* a PV array.

Array racks must be attached to the structural elements of a roof (trusses or rafters), and this will require penetrating the roofing surface material in a manner that is weatherproof for the life of the PV array or the life of the roof—whichever is shorter (photo 5-1).

Stainless steel hardware is usually used to connect the modules to the racks. Galvanized hardware is frequently used to bolt the racks to the roof. In both cases, corrosion resistance is a must in most climates.

PV Array—Cable Types and Installation

Electrically, the PV array consists of PV modules connected in series using the permanently attached, exposed single-conductor cables with "finger safe" connectors (photo 5-2). The conductors are typically USE-2 as allowed by *NEC* 690.31. In the *2008 NEC*, a

PHOTO 5.1 Array rack attachment point—used in dry climates

Chapter 5 — PV Modules

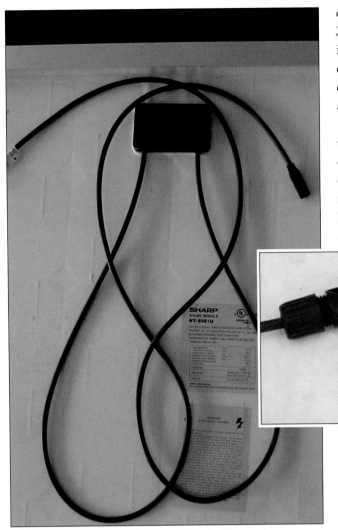

PHOTO 5.2 Module with attached cables and connectors

quirements in 690.33 for locking connectors in the *2008 NEC*. A tool will be required to open these locking connectors. They will also soon be appearing on most, if not all, PV modules, although they are only required when the PV array wiring is operating above 30 volts and is readily accessible (690.33).

Another *2008 NEC* requirement that applies to readily accessible PV source and output circuit conductors operating at over 30 volts is found in 690.31(A). These conductors must be installed in raceways. Unfortunately, most PV modules do not have junction boxes with knockouts that would accept a raceway. They come with permanently attached exposed, single-conductor cables and connectors with no provision for attaching a conduit or other raceway. Fortunately, most residential rooftop PV arrays are not readily accessible. A few manufacturers can provide conduit-ready modules on special order, but many module manufacturers have no such option.

The solution, as noted in the *2008 NEC Handbook*, is to make this wiring *not* readily accessible by placing some sort of barrier behind the modules that prevents the wiring from being touched without removing the barrier. Fences with locked gates may not be a solution, because a basic maintenance requirement for the readily accessible ground-mounted PV array is keeping the grass mowed—a task usually done by people not qualified to be near PV or other electrical systems.

The conductor leads attached to the modules are 40 inches long or longer to allow the series connection of modules when they are mounted in a landscape orientation (photo 5-3). When the modules are mounted in portrait orientation (photo 5-4), the excess lengths of conductors must be securely fastened against the module racks to resist abrasive damage due to wind, sleet, and ice. Many installers use plastic cable ties, but unless they are of very high quality, they may not last the required 40 years or more when exposed to the extremes of heat and ultraviolet radiation from sunlight. Some people use a stainless steel pipe clamp (loop strap) with an EDPM insert (photo 5-5).

new PV Wire (a.k.a. PV Cable, Photovoltaic Wire, or Photovoltaic Cable) is also allowed. This conductor is a "super" USE-2 that has a thicker jacket (the conduit fill tables cannot be used), passes a 720-hour accelerated UV test (is marked Sunlight Resistant), and has the flame and smoke retardants of RHW-2. It can be used under and within the PV array for the module interconnections and in raceways in other locations. This new cable will soon be appearing on all modules because it is required for the exposed cables on ungrounded PV arrays and the ungrounded array will facilitate the use of transformerless (also known as non-isolated) inverters (lower cost, less weight, higher efficiency) (*NEC* 690.35).

Although the electrical connectors attached to the ends of the module cables are "finger safe" when new, if they are opened under load, the dc arc may damage the insulation and the connectors may then pose a shock hazard. Therefore, there are new re-

PHOTO 5.3 Modules in landscape orientation

PHOTO 5.4 Modules in portrait orientation

PHOTO 5.5 Pipe clamp used to secure module conductors

Array Grounding

Section 690.47(D) [added in 2008; removed in 2011] requires that the PV array metal surfaces be connected directly to earth via a separate grounding electrode. This requirement provides a greater degree of lightning protection for PV systems than other *Code* requirements provide. This requirement was in addition to the normal equipment-grounding conductors that run with the circuit conductors and which are connected to earth (grounded) at locations remote from the PV array. If the array is on the same building that contains the inverter and the existing ac grounding electrode, then the array may be connected directly to that electrode and a separate electrode is not required (Ex. 1). If the connection to an existing electrode requires a horizontal extension greater than six feet from the closest

Chapter 5 — PV Modules

PHOTO 5.6 Grounding a metal roof — Oops, outdoor rated lug and wire needed

PV array should be connected to earth with equipment grounding conductors (photo 5-6). Rodent damage and abrasion of the conductor insulation could very well cause the module frames, the rack and/or the metal roof to be energized (photo 5-7).

The single-conductor exposed wiring (USE-2 or PV Wire) is allowed only in the near vicinity of the PV array to interconnect the modules and to return the end of the string conductor to the origination point of the string wiring. At this point, the exposed wiring must transition to one of the more common wiring methods found in Chapter 3 of the *Code*. Typically, this will be some form of conduit such as EMT. If the array output conductors penetrate the surface of the structure before reaching the first readily accessible dc PV disconnecting means, then they must be in a metal raceway where routed inside the structure. Metal raceways include rigid metal conduits (RMC), EMT, IMC, Metal Wireways and flexible metal conduit (FMC), and with the *2011 NEC*, include Type MC metallic cable assemblies. The transition fitting

earth contact point, a separate electrode is required (Ex. 2). This new array-grounding electrode does not have to be bonded to any other electrode (intent of the original submitter — the author).

Module grounding was covered in chapter 4 and will not be covered here in any detail. Suffice it to say that the module frames must be effectively grounded, and that is not always easy with aluminum frames and copper conductors. Those single-conductor exposed module circuit conductors are bound to touch the roof, if not on initial installation, sometime over the life of the system. The racks and any metal roofing panels under the

PHOTO 5.7 Rodent-damaged conductors

PHOTO 5.8 Cord grip transition. Can you spot the violation? [RMC threads differ from EMT threads.]

46   Photovoltaic Power Systems

> **Looking forward to 2014**
>
> 690.31 (A) was modified to indicate that the readily accessible exposed conductors operating over 30 V could be guarded. "Guarded" is defined in Chapter 1 of the code and it consists of providing mechanical protection so that these exposed conductors are not readily accessible.
>
> Section 690.47(D) has been reintroduced with added clarity.
>
> Section 690.8 was revised to require the correct calculation of ampacity when using conditions of use correction factors and adjustments.
>
> Section 310.15(B)(3)(c) applies the requirement for adding an additional temperature factor to "raceways and cables" exposed to sunlight on roofs. Cables indicate that not only module output conductors might be subject to solar heating, but also the output cables of microinverters. The 2011 *NEC* applied it only to "circular raceways".

keeps water, dirt, rodents, and other material out of the conduit. A rain head or a cord grip might be used (photo 5-8).

Ampacity Temperature Corrections

Modules can operate at very high temperatures (70–80 degrees C); the exposed wiring will come into contact with the hot surfaces; and the conductors originate in the hot termination boxes attached to the backs of the modules. Field-installed wiring (and the leads connected directly to the module) must be evaluated for temperature and ampacity corrections applied.

In most locations in the United States, a 75 degree C temperature correction factor is *suggested* for conductors near PV modules that are mounted roughly four inches or less from a surface like a roof. The distance in not exact and is normally measured from the back of the module frame to the surface. Four inches or less is insufficient clearance to allow much cooling air to flow behind the modules mounted in an array.

If the air space behind the modules is greater than four inches, then a 65 degree C temperature-

PHOTO 5.9 Conduits on hot roof

Chapter 5 — PV Modules

PHOTO 5.10 Conduit-ready PV module

correction factor is suggested. Again, these are not hard and fast numbers, and the individual installation location and microclimate (Death Valley or Nome) may affect them.

Conductors in conduit on roofs (and possibly elsewhere) in sunlight are also exposed to solar heating, and 310.15(B)(2) in the *2008 NEC* (310.15(B)(3) in *2011 NEC*) provides the temperature additions above the expected average high temperatures (photo 5-9). These temperatures apply not only to PV systems but to any conduits on the roofs of buildings exposed to sunlight. In many cases, where the high average temperatures are in the 40–45 degree range and the conduits are close (1/2" or less) to the roof, again a 65–75 degree C temperature correction factor might be used. Those PV circuit conductors are going to be delivering energy for the next forty years or more, so we really need to carefully apply these temperature correction factors to ensure that the insulation does not suffer premature degradation.

See Appendix D for examples of some of the math that must be used to calculate the ampacity of conductors in high temperatures and the open air as well as in conduit.

INSPECTORS and PLAN REVIEWERS

PLAN REVIEWERS:

Check frame grounding details and roof grounding details for metal roofs.

See if array racks are grounded for ground-mounted arrays or arrays on separate structures.

Verify that correct conductor types have been specified for ungrounded arrays.

INSPECTORS:

Verify grounding connections for modules, racks and roofs.

Verify correct conductor types and sizes.

Verify the use of metal raceways or metallic cable assembly for PV dc circuits inside the building.

Chapter 6

STILL ON THE ROOF

Aside from the PV modules, another component is frequently located on the roof. This is the PV source-circuit combiner and it will be followed in the dc circuit by the PV dc disconnecting means.

The PV Combiner

The PV source-circuit combiner is found on larger residential systems and on most large commercial systems. PV systems that have a dc rating above about 6 kW may have sufficiently large numbers of modules that more than two strings of modules are required to get the desired array power. Since module voltages range widely and module power ratings can vary from 40 watts to 300+ watts, there are no hard and fast rules relating the need for a dc combiner to a specific number of modules in an array.

PHOTO 6.1 PV source-circuit combiner with fuses

Multiple Strings May Need a Combiner

The rated output voltage of the PV modules and the inverter dc input characteristics determine how many modules may be connected in a series string. The power rating of each module and the number of modules in a string determine the power rating of a string. The desired array power rating and the power rating of the inverter determine how many strings need to be connected in parallel. Normally two strings can be connected in parallel without requiring a combiner containing overcurrent devices [690.9(A) Ex.]. If more than two strings are needed, then overcurrent protection on each string may be required and these overcurrent devices are placed in a PV source-circuit combiner.

A quick check on a smaller system (one with only one level of dc combiner boxes) is to compare the short-circuit current (I_{sc}) of the module with the number of strings that are to be connected in parallel. Find a number that is one less than the number of strings being connected in parallel. Multiply that number by 1.25 and by I_{sc}. If the result is more than

PHOTO 6.2 PV source-circuit combiner with circuit breakers—poor workmanship

PHOTO 6.3 PV source-circuit combiner on large system with improper color codes

the rating of the module protective fuse marked on the back of the module, then a fused combiner will be needed. As an example, a module has an I_{sc} of 6.5 amps, and three strings are going to be connected in parallel. The module has a series fuse rating of 15 amps. The number is 2 (3-1) and when the multiplications are done, 2 x 1.25 x 6.5 = 16.25. This is greater than 15, so fuses are needed in each of the source circuits before they are combined in the combiner. Sections 690.8 and 690.9 will require that the fuses be sized at a minimum of 1.25 x 1.25 x I_{sc} = 1.25 x 1.25 x 6.5 = 10.1 amps. The maximum fuse, based on the module markings, would be 15 amps, so a standard fuse of 12 or 15 amps could be used. See Appendix D for more details.

A combiner may use either fuses (typically on high-voltage, utility-interactive systems) or circuit breakers (used on systems operating at a nominal 48 volts or below). See photos 6-1, 6-2, and 6-3.

It should be noted that the combiners shown in photos 6-1 and 6-3 have exposed circuit terminals and busbars near the overcurrent devices. They are not dead front when opened, and voltages on the exposed terminals and busbars may approach 600 volts on many systems in cold weather. Although not dead front, these combiners *do meet* the intent of the *NEC*: where a tool is required to get access to energized surfaces (terminals and busbars). In these cases, the combiners have screw-on covers and the tool required to open the combiner is a screwdriver.

Chapter 6 — Still on the Roof

PHOTO 6.4 Dead-front PV source-circuit combiner   Courtesy of AMTec Solarv

The *2008 and 2011 NEC* require that combiners be listed and UL has determined that the listing must be to UL Standard 1741 (the PV inverter standard) [690.4(D)]. Although listing is required, UL 1741 has not yet been modified to specifically require that combiners be dead front. Some of the newer units are dead front, and eventually that requirement may be in the standard. See photo 6-4 of a dead-front unit that has terminal covers made of clear plastic.

Wiring from the PV Array to the PV Disconnect

Although the conductors between the modules and the return circuit from one end of a string to the other are permitted to be single conductor cables in free air, as soon as these circuits leave the array location they must transition to a standard *NEC* Chapter 3 wiring method. That wiring method must be suitable for the hot, wet environment found on roofs; and sunlight resistance is also a must for any exposed conductors. Electrical metallic tubing (EMT) is frequently used. The ampacity of the conductors is based on the short-circuit current being carried in that circuit and must be corrected for the conditions of use. In many cases, terminal temperature limitations on combiners or fused disconnects may dictate further conductor size corrections.

An equipment-grounding conductor should be run with the circuit conductors in the conduit. In the *2008 and 2011 NEC*, I_{sc} is used directly in Table 250.122 to select an equipment-grounding conductor. The reduction in size of the dc equipment-grounding conductor is due to the *2008 NEC* requirement that nearly all PV systems have ground-fault detectors that will limit ground-fault currents in the equipment-grounding conductors. On systems with PV source or output circuit fuses, the normal procedure of using the fuse value in Table 250.122 is used (690.45).

In many systems, the equipment-grounding conductors may be as small as 14 AWG between the PV modules based on the calculation above. However, in areas where winds, snow, ice and other environmental factors are significant, a larger equipment-grounding conductor should be considered to provide additional mechanical protection [690.46/250.120(C)]. Since the distances in open air between the modules are small, a 6 AWG, bare equipment-grounding conductor should be adequate for the most severe environmental circumstances. THHN-insulated green conductors should never be used in exposed outdoor locations for equipment grounding conductors.

The dc PV Disconnect

The dc PV disconnecting means (PV disconnect) should be installed in a readily accessible location, either inside or outside the building at the point of first penetration of the dc conductors (690.14) (photo 6-5). Since Section 690.31(E) allows the PV source or output conductors to penetrate the building surface on the roof (if they are routed in a metal raceway inside the building), it appears that the PV disconnect can be mounted inside the building in any readily accessible location. However, this *NEC* allowance may not be the safest option or even very clearly defined in the national *Code*.

This parallel wording of 690.14(C)(1) to the requirements for the ac service disconnecting means in 230.70(A)(1) may need further examination since in the world of ac utility-power, removal of the ac revenue meter can effectively disable the ac power in a structure where the ac service disconnect is inside a locked structure. With a dc PV disconnect inside a locked structure, the readily accessible defi-

Looking forward to 2014

DC combiner. A direct-current (dc) combiner has been defined and it includes all classes of combiners in the dc circuits. When discussing a specific combiner, the use of that combiner will have to be noted. Example: DC combiner (source circuit).

The dc combiner mounted on the roof must have a load break rated disconnect on its output or within 1.8 m (6 ft). It may be remotely controlled, but must have a manual operation capability [690.15(C)].

Section 690.9(D) requires that the overcurrent protection for PV source and PV output circuits be listed PV overcurrent devices.

A new section, **690.12 Rapid Shutdown of PV Systems on Buildings**, has been added. This section requires that any PV system circuit in or on a building operating at greater than 30 volts and 240 volt-amps must have a rapid shutdown system. At these or higher voltages or volt-amps, the circuits may be a maximum of 1.5 m (5 ft) in length inside a building and a maximum 3 m (10 ft) in length from a PV array on the outside of the building. This system will certainly affect the dc circuit conductors from the array output, the dc input circuits at the inverters which might be energized for up to five minutes at high voltages from internal energy storage devices, and the dc circuits associated with batteries above the voltage or volt–amp limits above. Any ac circuit above these limits would also be subjected to the rapid response requirement and that response time for reducing the voltages is 10 seconds after activation. First responders will be the ones to use this system and after the ac power is shut down to the structure to de-energize all non-PV ac circuits, the fast response system should ensure that all PV dc and ac circuits are de-energized if they are above 30 volts and 240 volt-amps.

The PV industry and potentially a new or modified UL Standard will determine how this system is to be implemented since it must be listed and identified for the application. External equipment may be used or modifications to existing products could meet the requirements. If dc combiners (source circuit) are within 3 m (10 ft) of the array and if they have the required remotely controlled dc output contactor, then that contactor might be used as part of the rapid shutdown system. Inverter input circuits might be internally modified to disconnect the external input terminals from the internal energy storage devices or an external contactor might be used.

Section 690.56(C) establishes specific and detailed plaque or directory requirements for buildings with Rapid Shutdown systems. These requirements include letter size 9.5 mm (3/8 in) and colors (white on red) and a reflective background.

nition may not be appropriate. Local jurisdictions may have requirements that exceed the minimum requirements of the *NEC*. Many jurisdictions require that the PV disconnect be located within sight of the ac service disconnect or meter on residences. This is usually on the outside of the building. On commercial buildings, the PV disconnect may be some distance from the ac service disconnect, and a directory may be used to show the location of all disconnects, both ac and dc (705.10).

The PV disconnect should break all ungrounded conductors, but *should not* open a grounded conductor. Grounded conductors in the dc circuits in PV systems may be either the negative or positive source-circuit conductors and should have white insulation, or where larger than 6 AWG, be marked with a white marking. The type of module used determines which circuit conductor should be grounded and the inverter must be compatible with that polarity of grounded conductor. The dc bonding jumper in a utility-interactive PV system is commonly inside the inverter and is a part of the ground-fault detection/interruption systems required by 690.5.

If the grounded source-circuit conductor *is* opened by the switch in the disconnect, the marked grounded conductor becomes *ungrounded* and may be energized with respect to ground up to the

PHOTO 6.5 PV dc disconnecting means

open-circuit voltage of the system. This represents an unsafe condition for people servicing the PV array and for that reason the *Code* prohibits the use of disconnects, breakers or fuses in grounded PV dc conductors, unless they are part of an automatic ground-fault detection/interruption system (690.13).

Photo 6-6 shows the front of a PV dc disconnect with the labels required by 690.17 and 690. 53. The 690.17 warning is required because the load terminals of this disconnect are connected to the inverter dc input which may be energized for up to five minutes after the disconnect has been opened. The filter and energy storage capacitors in the inverter will be discharged after this time. The 690.53 label with the system dc voltages and currents will allow the AHJ to determine if the correct cables, disconnects, and overcurrent devices have been installed.

Power flows in a PV system from the PV array through the dc PV disconnect, the inverter, the ac disconnect, and finally to

PHOTO 6.6 Disconnect labels

54   Photovoltaic Power Systems

PHOTO 6.7 Line and load terminals

the grid. This power flow sometimes confuses installers on how to properly connect the dc and ac disconnects. Note the upper line-side terminals on the disconnect shown in photo 6-7 are covered by an insulated cover. Also note the switchblades, the fuse holder terminals (if any), and the load-side lower terminals are exposed and easily touched. A general safety rule is that the most dangerous circuit should be connected to the protected, line-side terminals. If this is done, it is less likely that energized terminal connections will be accidentally touched when the door of the disconnect is open. In the PV dc disconnect, the PV source or output circuits should always be connected to the line-side terminals. The dc input to the inverter is connected to the load-side terminals and the 690.17 warning label is required as shown in photo 6-6. The dc input terminals are connected to energy storage capacitors inside the inverter and may be energized for up to five minutes. On the ac disconnect, the utility connection goes to the protected line side terminals at the top.

Summary

Attention to the *Code* requirements in 690 and other articles plus an understanding of PV equipment and how power flows in a PV system should enable these systems to be installed and operated in a safe manner. The utility-interactive inverter is next on our top to bottom tour of the PV system.

PHOTO 6.8 Solar Shutoff control box by Midnite Solar. Possible use to meet 2014 *NEC* 690.12 requirement.

INSPECTORS and PLAN REVIEWERS

PLAN REVIEWERS:

Verify that combiners are used where required and that they are listed devices.

Verify that all disconnects are drawn properly with the line side connected to the correct circuit and that the switch poles are on the load side.

Verify that the grounded dc circuit conductor is not broken by a switch, breaker or fuse unless part of a ground-fault device.

INSPECTORS:

Correct wiring methods used?

Conductors installed per the diagram?

Overcurrent devices with appropriate ratings?

Disconnects installed with the most dangerous circuit connected to the line side terminals?

Chapter 6 — Still on the Roof

Working safely on the roof requires the proper equipment and skills.

Chapter 7

Details, Details, Details

There are always a few details that get overlooked in designing, installing and inspecting these systems.

The Conductors

We have noted previously that single-conductor, exposed cables (type USE-2 or the new PV Cable/PV Wire) will be used for the module interconnecting cables. Both of these cable types will generally be available only in basic black. And, as 200.6(A)(6) notes, this black cable, even when smaller than 4 AWG, may be marked white as a grounded conductor at the time of installation where used as an exposed outdoor conductor at the array.

Normally the exposed single-conductor cables are transitioned to a conduit wiring method when the circuits leave the PV array. Conductors in conduit, while they could be USE-2/RHW-2 (for flame and smoke retardant) or PV Wire, are typically THHN/THWN-2 because they are less costly and the -2 rating is needed for the outdoor, wet environment and the high temperatures of conduit in sunlight [310.15(B)(3)]. Unfortunately, 14-10 AWG conductors with THHN/THWN-2 insulation are not widely available due to low demand. Of course THHN/THWN is available, but it doesn't have a wet, 90°C rating. Demand will increase for the small-conductor THHN/THWN-2 cables as inspectors start applying 310.15(B)(3) to rooftop HVAC installations. Due to the limited availability of 14-10 AWG THHN/THWN-2, XHHW-2 would be a suitable alternative.

Although most PV arrays installed in the recent past have had the dc negative conductor grounded (and colored white), newer arrays may have the dc positive conductor grounded and colored white. Of course, there are no designated color codes for the ungrounded conductor, but common sense would indicate that on a negatively grounded array with the negative conductor colored white, the positive, ungrounded conductor would be most clearly marked and understandable if it were colored red for conductors installed in conduit. However, many installations use a black positive conductor and that is still acceptable under the *Code*. In the positively grounded systems where the positive grounded conductor is colored white, the ungrounded negative conductor would be most clearly understood if it were black.

Now, and in increasing numbers in the next few years, the use of transformerless inverters will dictate the use of ungrounded PV arrays (690.35) and then we can go to a "red is positive" and "black is negative" color coding since there will be no grounded conductor. But, both ungrounded conductors can still meet *Code* if they are black.

Although not prohibited by the *Code*, the use of conductors with colored insulations in exposed outdoor conductors should be minimized since there is some question about their durability, even when listed as USE-2 or PV Wire, when exposed to UV radiation and high temperatures for decades.

Oh yes, we should not ignore the newest bipolar PV arrays and bipolar inverters. In these systems, we will have red, positive conductors, black, negative conductors, and white, grounded conductors. Of course, some installers will use black for both of the ungrounded conductors (acceptable under the *NEC*) and this will pose problems for the inspector and the troubleshooter when the cables are misconnected. The 2011 *NEC* has added numerous circuit marking, routing and grouping requirements in 690.4 and 690.31.

PHOTO 7.1 Enphase 175-watt micro inverter

As before, the grounded conductor in a PV dc disconnect should never be switched, although bolted, isolated, terminal-block connections are acceptable, but not required (690.13).

Wiring Methods—Continued

All circuits in a PV system, as in other electrical systems, must be wired using a Chapter 3 or a 690.31 method that is suitable for the application and the environment. However, there are frequently questions about the circuits between the dc PV disconnect and the inverter. As far as the *NEC* is concerned, if these circuits are in protected environments, they could be wired with type NM cable. Of course, local codes may dictate other requirements such as the need to use raceways inside commercial structures for all electrical wiring.

The Inverter

Utility-interactive inverters range in size from 175 watts (photo 7-1) to 1 megawatt and come in all shapes, sizes and colors (photos 7-2 and 7-3). New models are being introduced monthly. These inverters will be listed by UL, CSA, ETL, and TUV Rheinland, all of whom are designated as nationally recognized testing laboratories (NRTL) by OSHA for testing and listing PV modules, inverters, combiners, and charge controllers using standards published by UL.

Some inverters have only a single set of dc input terminals and no internal dc or ac disconnects. With these designs, an external dc PV disconnect must be installed. Even if the inverter has more than one set of input terminals for paralleling separate strings (source circuits) of modules, external dc PV disconnects must be used on each input (photo 7-4).

Other inverters have internal dc disconnects or disconnect housings that attach to the main inverter section containing the electronics package. The method used to mount the internal disconnects, the ease and accessibility of the disconnects, and the manner in which they are separated from the inverter proper vary from brand to brand and from product to product. The installer and the AHJ must reach a mutual conclusion on the suitability of these disconnects for meeting the various disconnect requirements in the *Code*.

PHOTO 7.2 Xantrex 100kW inverter

PHOTO 7.3 Emerson Industrial Automation 1.8 megawatt inverter

PHOTO 7.4 Solectria 13kW Inverter with external disconnects

PHOTO 7.5 Transformerless inverter with internal dc disconnect.

Since the inverters are listed with the disconnects, it can be presumed that the disconnects are properly rated for the dc load break operation. If the inverter were installed in a location that meets the 690.14 requirements for the main PV dc disconnect, then it would appear that the internal disconnect would meet this requirement.

Meeting the requirement for equipment disconnects (690.15) will require additional considerations. If the inverter were to require factory service, can the energized PV source or output circuits be disconnected from the inverter safely when there is no external disconnect? If a disconnect housing is attached to the inverter and that housing does not have to be removed to service the inverter, then some degree of safety is assured. However, if the energized conductors must be disconnected from internal switches and pulled through small conduit knockouts, the situation must be examined carefully. Will qualified people, who know how to disable the array, be doing the removal? Or will the unqualified person try to pull energized conductors through the knockouts? See photos 7-5 and 7-6.

Chapter 7 — Details, Details, Details

PHOTO 7.6 Inverter with internal disconnects that can be separated from inverter

PHOTO 7.7 PV combiner with disconnect at output

DC Input Fusing

Some models of both small (<10 kW) and large (>100 kW) inverters have dc input fuses mounted inside the inverter or inside a combiner/disconnect device attached to the inverter. The smaller fuses (30 amps or less) are usually mounted in "finger-safe" fuse holders that allow the fuse to be safely replaced in an un-energized (no load current) state.

However, when the fuse ratings go over 30 amps, with values as high as 400 amps or more, these fuses are mounted in exposed fuse holders or bolted directly to a dc busbar. One side of each fuse is tied together with the dc input of the inverter. The other side of each fuse is hardwired to the output of a PV dc combiner and these combiners will be scattered throughout the PV array—sometimes over acres of real estate. Although the inverter can be turned off and the dc input capacitors allowed to discharge (up to five minutes), each fuse is still energized from its own input and the combined inputs of all of the other fuses through the common bus bar. The only way to safely service these fuses is to go through the entire PV array, find all of the combiners, and open or pull each and every source circuit fuse (those less-than-30 amp "finger safe" fuse holders). An optional disconnect at the output of every combiner speeds this process and makes servicing the combiner fuses safer, but all disconnects must be located and opened (photo 7-7). Combiners are available with internal load-break rated output disconnects that, if used with a remote control, could speed the shutdown.

When these fuses are present in the input of the larger inverters, the safest way to provide for ser-

PHOTO 7.8 Disconnects for each input installed near the inverter

vice is to install a dc disconnect near the inverter on each dc input to a fuse (photo 7-8). These grouped disconnects can be easily opened, and with the inverter turned off, the fuses can be safely removed in a de-energized state. Section 690.16(B) has been revised to require dc disconnects near these fuses so that they can be safely de-energized from all sources when being serviced.

Equipment Grounding vs. DC System Grounding and DC Ground Faults

The *NEC* requires (with a few exceptions—see 690.35 and 690.41) that the dc portions of a PV system have a grounded circuit conductor and the dc part of the system becomes a grounded electrical system. In PV systems, a related requirement in 690.5 establishes that a dc ground-fault protection device be installed on most grounded PV systems. This ground-fault protection device is an integral part of the grounded PV dc system.

> ## Looking forward to 2014
>
> **Section 690.5** has a minor revision to require that ground faults be detected in intentionally grounded conductors. This requirement was added because ground faults as defined in Chapter 1 of the *Code* are between ungrounded conductors and grounded surfaces and this definition does not acknowledge the fact that ground faults in grounded conductors can also result in unwanted current that could contribute to fires. This is particularly important where supply circuits like PV systems or generators are involved and the main system bonding jumper is elsewhere in the system.
>
> **Section 690.11** concerning dc arc-fault circuit protection was slightly modified to ensure that only dc circuits were addressed and the requirement identifying specific equipment in (2) that should be disabled was removed.
>
> The extensive grouping, marking and identification requirements previously in 690.4 are now moved to 690.31.
>
> **Section 690.31(C)(2)** now permits any size of PV wire to be placed in cable trays in outdoor locations even when not marked for cable tray use. Support must be no less than 300 mm (12 inches) and securement must be no less than 1.4 m (4.5 feet).
>
> **Section 690.31(D)** allows a multiconductor cable (TC–ER, USE–2) to be used for the output conductors of utility interactive inverters located in not readily accessible areas. Cable shall be secured at 1.8 m (6 feet) intervals.
>
> **Section 690.31(G)(1)** establishes slightly revised marking requirements for PV circuits that are embedded in roofing membranes and that are not under the PV array.
>
> **Part III. Disconnecting Means.** This part has been substantially reorganized and revised and includes 690.13 through 690.18. The requirements of 690.14 have been moved to other sections. However, the requirements generally remain the same as in the 2011 *Code*.
>
> **Section 690.17** now allows power operable dc disconnecting means that have a manual operation capability. Numerous types of disconnecting means are listed in this section and there is some emphasis that they be suitable for interrupting current flow in both directions.
>
> **Section 690.35(C)** addressing ground-fault protection for ungrounded PV arrays was slightly modified in subparagraph (1) so that the intent is clear that ground faults are to be addressed in the PV array dc current-carrying conductors and components.

Ground-Fault Protection Devices

Section 690.5, Ground-Fault Protection, of the 1987 *National Electrical Code* added new requirements for photovoltaic (PV) systems mounted on the roofs of dwellings. The requirements are intended to reduce fire hazards resulting from ground faults in PV systems mounted on the roofs of dwellings. There is no intent to provide any shock protection for personnel, and the requirement is not to be associated with a direct current (dc) GFCI. The ground-fault protection device (GFPD) is intended to deal only with ground faults and not line-to-line faults.

The requirements for the ground-fault protection device have been modified in subsequent revisions of the *Code* and the current *2008 NEC* and *2011 NEC* requirements for the device are as follows.

- Detect a ground fault
- Interrupt the fault current
- Indicate that there was a ground fault
- Open the ungrounded PV conductors or disconnect or turn off the connected equipment

To understand how these GFPDs work, it must be understood that most currently available inverters, both stand-alone and utility-interactive, employ a transformer that isolates the dc grounded circuit conductor (usually the negative, but sometimes the positive) from the ac grounded circuit conductor (typically the neutral). With this transformer isolation, the dc side of a PV system may be considered to be *similar* to a separately derived system before the inclusion of the required GFPD. Note, this *similarity* to a separately derived ac system is *not*

Chapter 7 — Details, Details, Details

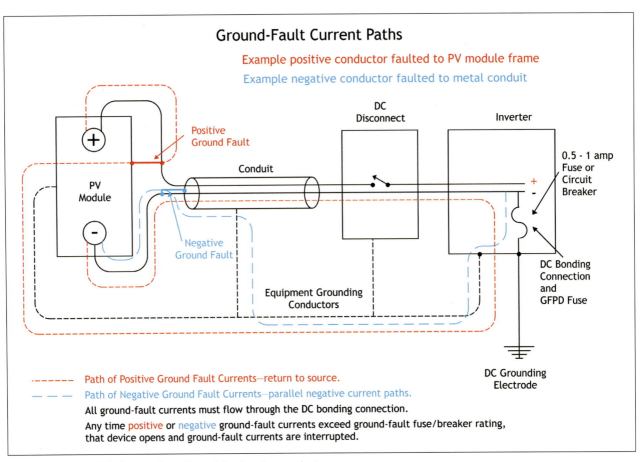

FIGURE 7.1 Ground-fault currents go through the bonding conductor.

sufficient to start applying 250.30 requirements to this dc system. The GFPD keeps one of the dc circuit conductors grounded and connected to the ac grounded circuit conductor through the grounding system. As such, there must be a single dc bonding connection (jumper) that connects the dc grounded circuit conductor to a common grounding point where the dc equipment-grounding conductors and the dc grounding electrode are connected. As in grounded ac systems, only a single dc bonding connection is allowed. If more than one bonding connection were allowed on either the ac side of the system or on the dc side of the system, unwanted currents would circulate in the equipment-grounding conductors and would violate *NEC 250.6*. The GFPD provides the dc bonding jumper.

GFPDs are available as separate devices for stand-alone PV systems and as internal circuits in most utility-interactive inverters. These devices contain and serve as the dc bonding connection.

In any ground-fault scenario on the dc side of the PV system, ground-fault currents from *any* source (PV modules or batteries in stand-alone systems) must eventually flow through the dc bonding connection on their way from the energy source through the fault and back to the energy source. This includes single ground faults involving the positive conductor faulting to ground or in the negative conductor faulting to ground. In ground faults involving the negative conductor (a grounded conductor), the fault creates unwanted parallel paths for the negative currents and the fault currents will also flow through the dc bonding connection. The diagram in figure 7-1 shows both positive (red) and negative (blue) ground faults and the paths that the fault currents take. As noted above, all ground-fault currents must pass through the dc bonding connection where the GFPD sensing device is located.

To meet the *NEC 690.5* requirements, a typical GFPD has a 1/2 amp to 1 amp and up to a 5 amp (on the larger inverters) overcurrent device installed in the dc bonding connection. When the dc ground-fault currents exceed the current rating of the device, it opens. By opening, the overcurrent device interrupts the ground-fault current as required in Section 690.5. If a circuit

PHOTO 7.9 Two-pole dc ground-fault detection and interruption circuit breaker assembly by Outback Power.

PHOTO 7.10 Utility-interactive inverter with GFPD. *Courtesy Fronius.*

breaker is employed as the overcurrent device, the tripped position of the breaker handle provides the indicating function. When a fuse is used, an additional electronic monitoring circuit in the inverter provides an indication that there has been a ground fault. The indication function is also an *NEC* 690.5 requirement. There is no automatic resetting of these devices.

In the GFPD using a circuit breaker as the sensing device, an additional circuit breaker is mechanically connected (common handle/common trip) to the sensing circuit breaker (photo 7-9). These types of GFPDs may be found in both stand-alone and 48-volt utility-interactive systems. This additional circuit breaker (usually rated at 100 amps and used as a switch rather than an overcurrent device) is connected in series with the ungrounded circuit conductor from the PV array. In this manner, when a ground-fault is sensed and interrupted, the added circuit breaker disconnects the PV array from the rest of the circuit, providing an additional indication that something has happened that needs attention.

Even though the GFPD uses a 100-amp circuit breaker in the ungrounded PV conductor, the 100-amp circuit breaker *should not* be used as the PV disconnect because in normal use of the system, turning off this breaker would unground the system and this is undesirable in non-fault situations. That action would also violate 690.13 requirements.

In the GFPD installed in utility-interactive inverters using a fuse as the sensing element, the electronic controls in the inverter that indicate that there has been a fault, also turn the inverter off and stop the power flow to the ac line. The inverters in photos 7-10 and 7-11 have internal fuses as part of the required ground-fault protection device. In listing these inverters, UL has indicated that this method of turning off the inverter to provide an additional indication of trouble meets the requirements of 690.5(B).

It should be noted that the dc GFPD detects and interrupts ground faults *anywhere* in the dc wiring, and the GFPD may be *located anywhere* in the dc system. GFPDs installed in the utility-interactive inverters or installed in dc power centers on stand-alone systems are the most logical places for these devices. There is no requirement to install them at the PV module location. Installing them at the modules would significantly increase the length of the dc grounding electrode conductor and complicate the routing of that conductor. To achieve significant additional safety enhancements would require a GFPD at each and every module. Equipment to do this does not exist and there are no requirements for such equipment.

Chapter 7 — Details, Details, Details

PHOTO 7.11 3kW utility-interactive inverter with GFPD. *Courtesy SMA Technology AG*

These devices are fully capable of interrupting ground faults occurring anywhere in the dc system including faults at the PV array or anywhere in the dc wiring from the PV module to the inverter and even to the battery in stand-alone systems. All of this can be done from any location on the dc circuit. Fire reduction and increased safety are achieved by having these GFPD on residential PV systems. Research is underway to evaluate other ground-fault detection circuits to determine if they may add an additional degree of safety for both single and multiple ground faults.

Yes, during a ground-fault, the dc bonding connection is opened, and if the ground fault cures itself for some reason, the dc system remains ungrounded until the system is reset. A positive-to-ground fault may allow the negative conductor (now ungrounded) to go to the open-circuit voltage with respect to ground. This is addressed by the marking requirements of Section 690.5(C). A very high value resistance is usually built into the GFPD and this resistance bleeds off static electric charges and keeps the PV system loosely referenced to ground (but not solidly grounded) during ground-fault actions. The resistance is selected so that any fault currents still flowing are only a few milli-amps—far too low to be a fire hazard.

The *2011 NEC* brings the DC PV Arc-Fault Circuit Interrupter

Section 690.11, new to the *2011 NEC*, establishes the requirement for a device that will detect a series arc in the dc PV source and output conductors and interrupt that arc. Parallel arcs are not addressed since it was determined that aging modules and connections throughout the PV system posed a more immediate risk. The requirement addresses the detection, interruption, disablement or disconnection and annunciation functions. The devices started appearing in the market in early 2011 and will appear in utility-interactive inverters, in charge controllers, and as separate devices located at the inverter, at the combiner, and possibly even at each individual module.

Summary

A detailed understanding of PV equipment and how power flows in a PV system should enable better, more thorough inspections of these systems. Better inspections will result in better, safer PV installations. We will continue with more information on the utility-interactive inverter in the next chapter.

INSPECTORS and PLAN REVIEWERS

PLAN REVIEWERS:

Correct conductor types and sized used?

Disconnects meet local and *NEC* requirements?

Switches connected properly?

Verify that the system has a ground-fault protection device either built into the inverter or charge controller (see equipment manual) or as a separate piece of equipment.

INSPECTORS:

Color codes?

Conductors properly terminated?

Disconnects in the correct locations?

Labels for ground-fault activation?

Chapter 8

THE INVERTER OPERATION & CONNECTIONS

The utility-interactive inverter is a key element in the PV system that helps to ensure safe and automatic operation of the system while converting the energy from the sun into useful electrical power.

Peak Power Tracking

A PV array is a current source of energy and the output power depends on the load that the inverter places on the array. No loading (zero current) would operate the array at the open-circuit voltage point (V_{oc}), and the heaviest loading (a short-circuit, hard to achieve) would operate the array at the short-circuit current (I_{sc}) point. Neither of these operating points would produce any power output from the array. Power being the product of voltage and current and at these points, one of them is zero. However, for every condition of sunlight intensity (irradiance) and array temperature, there is a load that will extract the maximum power from

PHOTO 8.1 Backfed PV breakers at bottom of busbar

the array that the array can produce under those conditions. The utility-interactive inverter will find that maximum or peak power point — maximum power voltage (V_{mp}) and maximum power current (I_{mp}) — and track that point as the sunlight and temperature vary throughout the day. See chapter 2 for more information.

Automatic Operation

Today's utility-interactive (U-I) inverter is designed, manufactured, tested and certified/listed to operate automatically in the PV system. There are no transfer switches. The inverter seamlessly converts dc power from the PV array into ac power that is fed into the utility-supplied premises wiring system. The output of the inverter is functionally connected in parallel with the premises wiring (and loads) and the utility service.

One of the most important aspects of the inverter is the anti-islanding circuit. The anti-islanding circuit is designed to keep the utility electrical system (both premises wiring and utility feeder) safe in the event that the utility is being serviced or is disconnected at some point in the transmission system, distribution system or premises wiring system.

Unlike the engine-driven generator, which can feed power into a blacked out/disconnected local utility feeder system, the inverter anti-islanding system prevents the inverter from energizing the "dead" power system.

This circuit prevents the inverter from delivering ac power if the utility voltage and frequency are not present, or if they are not within narrowly defined limits. This circuit monitors the voltage and frequency at the output terminals of the inverter. If the voltage varies more than plus ten percent or minus twelve percent from the nominal output voltage the inverter is designed for (120, 240, 208, 277, or 480 volts), the inverter cannot send power to the output terminals. Nor, is there any voltage on these terminals (from the inverter) when the inverter shuts down. In a similar manner, if the frequency varies from 60 Hz more than 60.5 Hz or less than 59.3 Hz, the inverter also cannot send power to the ac output. If the utility power is suddenly not present at the output terminals for any reason (inverter ac output disconnect opened, service disconnect opened, meter removed from the socket, utility maintenance, or utility blackout), the inverter senses this and immediately ceases to send power to the output terminals.

The anti-islanding circuit in the inverter continues to monitor the ac output terminals and when the voltage and frequency from the utility both return to specifications for a period of five minutes, the inverter is again able to send PV power to the ac output. When the inverter is not processing dc PV power into ac output power, it essentially stops taking power from the PV array by moving the load on the PV array to a point where there is no power. Usually this is the V_{oc} point for the PV array.

Circuit Sizing

DC

The dc input circuit and conductors to the inverter are sized based on the dc short-circuit current in those conductors and that sizing is covered in previous chapters and appendix D. There is no direct relationship, or code requirement, between the array rated output current and the manufacturer's specified maximum dc inverter input current. Normally the PV array is rated in watts at standard test conditions (STC) of 1000 watts per square meter (W/m^2) of irradiance and a cell temperature of 25 degrees Celsius (°C). In most cases, the array will operate, on average, at a lower power output due to the normal and expected power lost due to module heating. For this reason, inverter manufacturers typically suggest sizing the PV array (STC dc watts) at ten to twenty percent greater than the inverter ac power output rating. It does no short-term harm to connect an even larger PV array to the inverter since the inverter must limit its output to the rated value no matter how much array power is applied. If this over-sized array is used, the inverter will spend more operating time each day at rated power output than it would with a smaller array. The penalty for designing a system in this manner will be increased module cost for the larger array, some lost power on sunny, cool days, and possibly some slight reduction in the inverter life due to longer operation at full-power higher internal temperatures.

AC

The ac output circuit of an inverter must be sized at 125 percent of the rated output current of the inverter (690.8). Some inverter manufacturers specify the rated current or a range of values (due to vary-

PHOTO 8.2 GFP breaker. To backfeed or not? Only the manufacturer knows.

ing line voltages from nominal). If this specification is not given, then the rated power may be divided by the nominal line voltage to determine a rated current. For example, a 2500-watt inverter operating at a nominal voltage of 240 volts would have a rated current of

    2500 watts/240 volts = 10.4 amps

These inverters are not capable of providing any sustained (more than a second) surge currents, so the rated output current is all that can be delivered. When faced with a short-circuit, the rated output current is all that can be delivered, but more than likely, the reduced line voltage due to the fault will cause the inverter to shut down.

Connections
Dedicated Circuit
NEC 690.64(B)(1)/705.12(D)(1) requires that the inverter output be connected to the utility power source at a dedicated disconnect and overcurrent protective device (OCPD). In most systems this is a backfed breaker in a load center/panel board [690.64(B)/705.12(D)]. Inverters may not have their outputs connected directly to another inverter or directly to an ac utility-supplied circuit without first being connected to the dedicated disconnect/OCPD. The utility-interactive microinverters and the ac PV module are an exception to this rule since they are tested and listed to have multiple inverters connected in parallel on a single circuit with only one OCPD/disconnect device for an entire set of inverters. Chapter 10 and Appendix E have more details on the requirements found in 690.64(B)/705.12(D) from the 2011 *NEC* and earlier editions. Appendix H has a detailed look at the changes in 705.12(D) in the 2014 *NEC*.

The OCPD must be sized at a minimum of 125% of the rated inverter output current (or total of the output-rated output current from multiple micro inverters or ac PV modules) and it must protect the circuit conductor from overcurrents from the utility side of the connection. It is usually *not* a good idea to install a larger OCPD than the minimum required value (allowing a round up to the next standard value is okay and needed) because the inverter may, as part of the listing/instructions, be using the OCPD to protect internal circuits. The maximum value of allowable overcurrent device should be in the inverter instruction manual and should not be exceeded, 110.3(B).

Where fused or unfused disconnects are used for the ac inverter output disconnect, (or the required utility disconnect), the circuit connected to the utility source should be connected to the supply side (top) of the disconnect with the inverter ac output connected to the load side (bottom). No 690.17 warning label is required, because when the disconnect is opened, the inverter ceases to produce power within a fraction of a second and the exposed load-side terminals pose no shock hazard.

Is It a Branch Circuit?
Consider the typical indoor residential branch circuit.

    1. The branch circuit is protected by an OCPD at the source of power (the utility) *that can damage the circuit* (emphasis added).

    2. If the breaker protecting the branch circuit is opened, the circuit becomes completely "dead" (de-energized).

    3. If the branch circuit has a solid ground fault

PHOTO 8.3 Module/array conductors must be rated for outdoor conditions and secured properly.

or a line-to-line fault, the OCPD will open and protect the conductors.

4. The branch circuit may be wired with Type NM cable in residential applications.

Although not defined as a branch circuit, let us consider the circuit between the utility-interactive inverter ac output and the dedicated disconnect/OCPD (usually a breaker).

1. This circuit is protected by an OCPD at the source of power (the utility) that can damage it. Since the circuit is sized at 125 percent of the rated output current of the inverter and the inverter current is limited to the rated current, the inverter is not a source of current that can damage the conductor.

2. If the breaker protecting this circuit is opened, the circuit becomes completely "dead" (de-energized).

3. If this circuit has a solid ground fault or a line-to-line fault, the OCPD will open and protect the conductors. And the inverter will shut down.

4. It would appear in every practical sense that this utility-interactive inverter ac output circuit is just like a branch circuit and it, too, may be wired with Type NM cable in residential applications.

These ac output circuits from the utility-interactive inverters can be wired like any other branch circuit in a residence. These circuits, in a dwelling, do not need to be placed in a metal raceway as do the dc circuits between the modules and the dc PV disconnect. Of course, the inverters are surface-mounted devices and there may be the possibility of exposed Type NM cables being subject to physical damage. If they are, then conduit or other wiring method would be required.

The metal raceway requirement of 690.31(E) applies only to the always-energized dc PV source and dc PV output circuits,

Flush-mounted inverters are starting to appear on the market, and they will have a ventilation system to remove the internal heat generated during the inverting process.

GFCIs and AFCIs

The ac output of a utility-interactive inverter *should not* be connected to a GFCI (ground-fault circuit interrupter) or AFCI (arc-fault circuit interrupter) circuit breaker, as these devices are not currently

Chapter 8 — The Inverter Operation & Connections

designed to be backfed and will be damaged if backfed. These devices have terminals marked "line" and "load" and have not been identified/tested/listed for backfeeding.

Ground-Fault Protection on Main Breakers

The *NEC* has had, for many editions, a requirement (230.95) that solidly grounded wye services rated at 150–600 volts phase-to-phase and 1000 amps or more have ground-fault protection. Connecting a PV inverter ac output on the load side of these GFP equipped main breakers may pose safety issues.

Circuit breakers are manufactured with numerous optional accessories including— depending on manufacturer and model—shunt trips, auxiliary switches, remote indicators, power operation, adjustable trips, and ground-fault protection (GFP) trip mechanisms. While UL Standard 489 requires tests for evaluating the backfeed suitability of the basic circuit breaker, most of the accessories are not evaluated for backfeeding. In fact, backfeeding may have no affect on many of these accessories, and specific testing for backfeeding may be unnecessary.

However, older and possibly some current ground-fault trip mechanisms may be damaged if the circuit breaker has voltages on both line and load terminals after the breaker has been opened by a ground-fault trip. UL 489 testing does not evaluate backfed GFP main breakers in a manner that subjects the ground-fault device to the conditions it would experience in a utility-interactive PV system or possibly even in a parallel-connected generator installation where line and load terminals are both energized during and after a ground-fault trip. PV inverters may have energized outputs up to two seconds after the ac utility power is removed from the output.

Circuit breaker manufacturers should be evaluating all accessories supplied with their breakers for operation under all possible application configurations. However, utility-interactive inverter installations are relatively new applications and the inverters are being installed in electrical installations that may be decades old.

Informal discussions with manufacturers indicate that most new designs use a current transformer to power the GFP device, and that current transformer does not respond to the voltages on a tripped open main breaker. The GFP device, powered by the current transformer, should not be damaged by backfeeding.

However, there is some confusion and uncertainty about the older GFP/breaker designs that are installed widely and may still be on the market.

In the *2008 and 2011 NEC*, Sections 690.64(B)(3)/705.12(D)(3) and the Exception listed there require that the *ground-fault protection device* be identified and listed for backfeeding. Those ground-fault devices are not specifically tested and listed under UL Standard 489 requirements.

Only the breaker manufacturer (design engineer) can verify that the particular breaker with GFP by part number and model number will not be damaged under PV inverter backfed conditions (both line and load terminals energized at the same time during and after the GFP device trips the breaker). Bulletins and information from the sales departments are usually insufficient to make a determination.

After determining that the main breaker/GFP is suitable, then the issue of protecting the load circuits under ground-fault conditions from all sources, utility and PV must be addressed [690.64(B)(3) Exception/705.12(D)(3) EX]. An engineering analysis would be required that shows how and where ground-fault currents are sourced. What are the impedances involved in the utility source and the PV source and how much current can each supply under varying types of ground faults? Ground faults are not always "hard" low-resistance faults and may be arcing faults of varying impedances. Suppose the PV system sources enough ground-fault current to prevent the main breaker GFP from tripping? How is the ground fault contained or interrupted?

Some manufacturers are wary of putting some sort of GFP device on the inverter output because this is a non-standard connection and any ground faults detected might only be those originating between the device and the inverter, not load ground faults.

Some manufacturers have a main breaker GFP that can take inputs from multiple ground-fault

> ### Looking forward to 2014
>
> **Section 705.12(D)** has been revised extensively and is covered in some detail in Appendix H.

sources like a dual utility feeder systems. But these would be found in limited, special instances where there are multiple utility feeds.

Summary: The requirements of the *NEC* are stringent, but can be met. There are no one-size-fits-all solutions to this issue. The following steps should be followed before connecting a PV system that could backfeed a GFP breaker. There may be others.

1. Accurately determine that any and all ground-fault protection devices are suitable for operation in a backfed manner with a utility-interactive PV inverter.

2. Select an appropriate GFP device(s) that can be connected to the inverter(s) outputs to control ground-fault currents from that source.

3. Make an engineering assessment of the magnitudes of the potential and available fault currents from both utility and PV sources to the load circuits being protected. Circuit impedance calculations under fault current levels for all sources and the load impedance should be made.

4. Determine the proper setting for all adjustable trip ground-fault protection devices that will ensure that the load circuits are protected from all ground-fault current sources.

5. With the GFP breaker being back fed with current from the PV inverter, the GFP device should be tested using the internal test device. It should be tested a second time to ensure that the device was not damaged during the first test.

In many cases, it may be easier to implement a supply-side (of the main GFP breaker) PV connection as allowed by 690.64(A)/705.12(A)/230.2(A)(5)/230.82(6). These connections will be discussed in a later chapter.

Summary

A detailed understanding of PV equipment and how power flows in a PV system should enable better, more thorough inspections of these systems. Better inspections will result in better, safer PV installations.

> ## INSPECTORS and PLAN REVIEWERS
>
> **PLAN REVIEWERS:**
>
> **Verify** that the inverters are listed to UL 1741.
>
> **Determine** that there are no AFCIs, GFCIs or main breakers with GFP devices that may be subject to backfeed currents from the PV system.
>
> **Suggest** that a professional engineer stamp the plans if the back fed main breaker has a GFP device.
>
> **Verify** conductor sizing for inverter ac output circuits and the rating of the OCPD protecting this circuit.
>
> **INSPECTORS:**
>
> **Verify** that the inverter is on a dedicated circuit.
>
> **Verify** correct conductor sizes per the plan.
>
> **Check** for the presence of a GFP-protected main breaker.

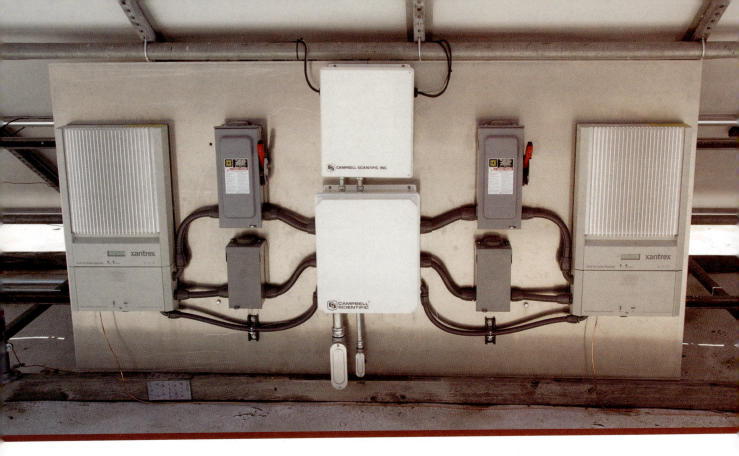

Chapter 9

Grounding the Inverter and the PV Array

Connecting the utility-interactive inverter and the PV array properly is critical to the safe, long-term, and reliable operation of the entire system. Proper grounding of the inverter and the array will minimize the possibility of electrical shocks and damage from surge currents. Understanding and applying the requirements of *NEC* 690.47 to the inverter and additional array grounding connections is somewhat complex but ensures that the user will be safe and that the inverter and other equipment will suffer minimum damage under surge conditions.

Equipment Grounding Conductors

In a typical residential or small commercial PV system (less than about 20 kW), the inverter serves as a central focal point for grounding connections. The dc equipment grounding conductor from the PV array and the dc disconnect are connected to the inverter. The ac inverter output circuit equipment grounding conductor leading to the point of connection with the utility is connected to the inverter. Under the *2005 NEC* and earlier editions of the *Code*, the dc equipment grounding conductors may be the only connection the module frames have to earth. UL Standard 1741 for PV inverters and charge controllers, quoted in part below, requires equipment grounding terminals in the inverter for both the ac and dc circuits.

> 18.1.8 Equipment grounding leads or equipment grounding terminals shall be provided for each input and each output circuit.

DC Grounding-Electrode Terminal

Most utility-interactive inverters installed as of early 2012 employ transformers, are connected to grounded PV arrays, and have an internal ground-fault indication/detection (GFID) system (690.5). This GFID system includes the internal bonding jumper between the dc grounded conductor and the grounding system. The presence of this dc bonding jumper requires, according to UL Standard 1741, that the inverter have a dc grounding electrode terminal. Here is what UL Standard 1741 requires (in part) for the dc grounding-electrode terminal. Italics added by the author.

> 18.2.1 Equipment intended to be installed as service entrance equipment or equipment containing the *main dc* or ac *bonding connection* shall be provided with a grounding electrode terminal.

These grounding connection requirements will require that each inverter have a minimum of three terminals available for making the proper connections. There will be terminals for the ac and dc equipment grounding conductors (at least two) and one for the dc grounding electrode conductor. All three terminals may be on a common bus bar or mounted separately in the inverter. They will normally all be connected (bonded) together electrically in the inverter, and they will be connected to the inverter chassis. If the inverter has multiple dc input circuits or an internal combiner, there should be a dc equipment grounding conductor terminal for each input (photos 9-1, 9-2 and 9-3).

To ensure proper grounding of the entire PV system, it is necessary to connect all three of these terminals properly. Because other countries do not ground PV systems like our *Code* requires, some inverters get certified/listed without a dc grounding-electrode terminal. The Europeans use the term *protective earth* (PE) terminal instead of equipment grounding terminal. Some inverters have only one equipment grounding terminal, not the required two and may not even have a grounding-electrode conductor terminal (photo 9-4).

Some inverters have an external grounding electrode terminal and the equipment grounding conductors are permanent leads coming out of the inverter (photos 9-5 and 9-6).

When the installer or inspector finds one of these inverters with missing grounding terminals, the manufacturer and the listing agency should be contacted. It is possible, in many cases, to splice the ac and dc equipment grounding conductors together and connect them

PHOTO 9.1 Three grounding terminals on bus bar

Chapter 9 — Grounding the Inverter and the PV Array

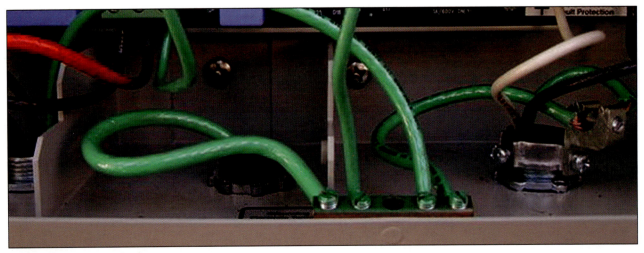

PHOTO 9.2 Grounding bus bar

to a single equipment grounding terminal. However, the dc grounding-electrode conductor must be connected directly to the proper terminal and should not be spliced.

690.47(C) — Connecting the Inverter to Ground (Earth)

The *Code* had significant changes between the 2005, 2008 and 2011 editions in Section 690.47(C) that addresses the dc grounding electrode connection. As far as the author can determine, either the permissive requirements of this section in the *2005 NEC* or the permissive requirements in the *2008 NEC* may be applied to connect the grounding-electrode conductor when installing a system in jurisdictions using either *Code*. A revision of 690.47(C) in the *2011 NEC* includes all three methods and has improved clarity. Note that sections 690.47(C)(1) and (2) on page 74 align with 690.47(C)(1) and 690.47(C)(2) in the *2005 NEC* and section 690.47(C)(3) aligns with 690.47(C) in the *2008 NEC*. Reviewing this revised *Code* section (shown below) may assist the reader in understanding the existing 690.47(C) in the 2005 and 2008 *Codes*.

PHOTO 9.3 Three grounding terminals

PHOTO 9.4 Only one equipment grounding terminal (PE) and no grounding electrode conductor terminal

690.47(C) Systems with Alternating and Direct Current Grounding Requirements. PV systems having direct current (dc) circuits and alternating current (ac) circuits with no direct connection between the dc grounded conductor and ac grounded conductor shall have a dc grounding system. The dc grounding system shall be bonded to the ac grounding system by one of the methods listed in (1), (2), or (3).

This section shall not apply to ac PV modules.

When using the methods of (2) or (3), a visual inspection shall be made to ensure that the existing ac grounding-electrode system meets the applicable requirements of Article 250, Part III.

Informational Note No. 1: ANSI/Underwriters Laboratory Standard 1741 for PV inverters and charge controllers requires that any inverter or charge controller that has a bonding jumper between the grounded dc conductor and the grounding system connection point have that point marked as a grounding-electrode conductor (GEC) connection point. In PV inverters, the terminals for the dc equipment grounding conductors and the terminals for ac equipment grounding conductors are generally connected to, or electrically in common with, a grounding busbar that has a marked dc GEC terminal.

Informational Note No. 2: For utility-interactive systems, the existing premises grounding system serves as the ac grounding system.

PHOTO 9.5 External grounding electrode terminal

(1) Separate DC Grounding Electrode System Bonded to the AC Grounding Electrode System. A separate dc grounding electrode or system shall be installed, and it shall be bonded directly to the ac grounding-electrode system. The size of any bonding jumper(s) between ac and dc systems shall be based on the larger size of the existing ac grounding-electrode conductor or the size of the dc grounding electrode conductor specified by 250.166. The dc grounding electrode system conductor(s) or the bonding jumpers to the ac grounding electrode system shall not be used as a substitute for any required ac equipment grounding conductors.

(2) Common DC and AC Grounding Electrode. A dc grounding-electrode conductor of the size specified by 250.166 shall be run from the marked direct-current grounding electrode connection point to the ac grounding-electrode. Where an ac grounding electrode is not accessible, the dc grounding-electrode conductor shall be connected to the ac grounding-electrode conductor in accordance with 250.64(C)(1). This dc grounding-electrode conductor shall not be used as a substitute for any required ac equipment grounding conductors.

(3) Combined DC Grounding Electrode Conductor and AC Equipment Grounding Conductor. An unspliced, or irreversibly spliced, combined grounding conductor shall be run from the marked dc grounding-electrode conductor connection point along with the ac circuit conductors to the grounding bus bar in the associated ac equipment. This combined grounding conductor shall be the larger of the size specified by 250.122 or 250.166 and shall be installed in accordance with 250.64(E).

While any of the three methods of making connections to the inverter grounding electrode terminal may be used, there are advantages and disadvantages to each.

Method (1), noted above, similar to 690.47(C)(1) in the *2005 NEC*, has the advantage of routing surges picked up by the array more directly to earth than methods (2) and (3). However, since a new bonding conductor between the new dc grounding electrode and the existing premises ac grounding electrode is required, there is the size, routing and cost of that conductor to consider.

Method (2) [similar to 690.47(C)(2) in the *2005 NEC*] uses fewer components than the other two methods and also routes surges to earth without getting near the ac service equipment.

Depending on the types of grounding electrodes being used, the bonding jumper size will have to meet the requirements of 250.66 or 250.166 whichever yields the largest size.

Method (3) [similar 690.47(C) in the *2008 NEC*] combines the inverter ac equipment grounding con-

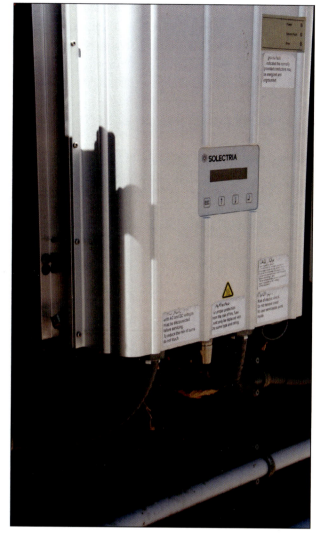

PHOTO 9.6 Equipment grounding conductors as leads attached to the inverter and routed in conduit

Grounding the PV Array: 690.47(D) [2008 NEC only]

In addition to the required equipment grounding conductors from the PV module frames and mounting rack to the inverter that run in the raceways with the circuit conductors, the *NEC* now requires that the PV array, in some cases, also be connected directly to ground (earth).

The intent of the original proposal (submitted by the author) for 690.47(D) was to highlight, in Article 690, a permissive (optional) array grounding method along the lines of the permissive auxiliary grounding electrodes described in 250.54 and was intended to serve as a method of reducing damage from surges induced by lightning. The intent of the proposal was to not require this array-grounding electrode to be bonded to any other electrode in concert with the methods of 250.54.

However, the code-making process does not always get the language or intent clear when the *Code* is finally published and we have to do the best with what we have. This section of the *Code* was removed from the *2011 NEC*.

Section 690.47(D) requires that ground- or pole-mounted PV arrays have a grounding electrode conductor between the module frames and racks and ground (earth).

Since the utility-interactive inverter is considered a load for the PV array, if it is on a different structure from the array, then the array should be grounded directly to earth with a grounding electrode conductor. This concept of *separation* of the array from the inverter is extracted or interpreted from the term *integral* in Exception 1. Very few PV arrays have the load integral with the array, and even systems with microinverters may have the inverter integral with the module, not the array. So, it appears if the load and the PV array are on the same structure then there is no *Code* requirement for this additional array grounding system.

However, following the intent of reducing damage from nearby lightning strikes, a recommendation can be made that all PV arrays in high lightning regions of the country have this direct grounding path from the array to earth.

What about Exception No. 2? Electrical surges

ductor with the dc grounding electrode conductor and thereby uses less copper. However, the requirement to bond the conductor at the entrance and exit of each metallic conduit and enclosure, to minimize the inductive choke effect, may become difficult with conductor sizes greater than about 6 AWG, especially since the conductor must remain unspliced or irreversibly spliced. Also, any surges picked up by the array will be routed directly to the service equipment and may be more likely to enter the premises wiring system than when grounding electrode conductors are routed more directly to ground.

The grounding busbar in the ac equipment where this combiner conductor terminates should also be where an existing grounding electrode routed to a grounding electrode terminates. The combined conductors should not terminate on a grounding bus bar that is not connected directly to earth.

> ## Looking forward to 2014
>
> Numerous non-isolated inverters are coming to the market. These are also known as transformerless inverters and are designed to be used with ungrounded PV arrays where neither the positive nor negative array conductor is connected to ground. Of course, the arrays and the inverters both have equipment grounding conductor requirements. UL Standard 1741 requires that terminals be provided for equipment grounding conductors (EGC) for each input or output. A terminal is also required for a grounding electrode conductor (GEC) if there is an internal bond between one of the circuit conductors and ground. Since these non-isolated inverters do not have any such bond, there is no requirement for a grounding electrode conductor terminal. However, some of the European manufacturers and even some of those in the United States are not fully familiar with the requirements of the standards and they have placed a GEC terminal on their non-isolated inverters. If such a terminal appears on the inverter it must be connected to a grounding electrode conductor, which is in turn routed and connected to ground (earth) according to code requirements. This is required because *NEC* Section 110.3(B) requires that any labels or instructions provided with the listed product be followed.
>
> **Section 690.47(D)** was returned to the 2014 *Code* with some slight revisions for additional clarity. Directly grounding the array (modules and rack) is now required in many installations in addition to the equipment grounding conductor system.

due to lightning like to go in straight lines. If the grounding electrode conductor from the PV array can get to earth within six feet of an existing premises grounding electrode, then that electrode can be used to meet this requirement. A horizontal run longer than six feet to reach an existing electrode would require placing a new electrode.

Summary

Proper grounding connections at the inverter and to the PV array are critical to a safe and properly operating PV system. These connections may be the only connections that the entire system has to earth. All connections must be made and that may prove difficult if manufacturers have not included the proper number of terminals. Good grounding and bonding practices may help to reduce equipment damage from light-induced surges.

In the next chapter, we will cover the ac output circuits of the utility-interactive inverter.

> ## INSPECTORS and PLAN REVIEWERS
>
> **PLAN REVIEWERS:**
> **Ensure** that the dc and ac equipment conductors are shown properly and are properly sized.
>
> **Verify** that a dc grounding electrode conductor is routed properly from the inverter to a grounding electrode, or to a grounding busbar, where a grounding electrode conductor connected to a grounding electrode terminates.
>
> **INSPECTORS:**
> **Ensure** that the inverter has the proper grounding terminals and that they are connected as required.
>
> **Each conductor** to the grounding electrode should have a separate clamp.
>
> **Grounding electrode conductors** should be unspliced, or if spliced, the splicing method should be irreversible such as a crimp splice of exothermic welding.
>
> **Grounding electrode conductors** run through metallic raceways or enclosures should be bonded to the metal raceways or enclosures at entry and exit points.

Chapter 10

Load-Side AC Utility Connections

Connecting the utility-interactive inverter to the utility grid properly is critical to the safe, long-term, and reliable operation of the entire system. The ac output circuit requirements and the circuits that carry the inverter current in the premises wiring are somewhat complex. However, meeting *Code* requirements can and should be accomplished to ensure a safe and durable system.

Inverter Output Circuit

In general, the output circuit on an inverter to the first overcurrent device should be sized at 125% of the rated output current of the inverter that, in turn, is determined from the specifications or by dividing the rated power by the nominal ac output voltage. For example, a 2500-watt, 240-volt inverter will have a rated output current of:

PHOTO 10.1 There must be an open space somewhere.

$2500/240 = 10.4$ amps

$1.25 \times 10.4 = 13.02$.

These requirements appear in 690.8. A 15-amp circuit breaker is the next larger standard size and at least 14 AWG conductors should be used. In a few cases, the inverter manufacturer may specify a higher rated current based on a lower than nominal operating voltage (the low end of the anti-islanding range) and this value of rated current should be used. Voltage drop and conditions of use may require a larger conductor. Higher rated overcurrent devices should not normally be used; even though they may be appropriate for the conductor being used, they may not provide required protection for internal inverter circuits. The inverter manual will generally specify the maximum allowable overcurrent device rating.

Even though power and current flow from the inverter to the utility, it should be noted that the utility-end of this circuit is where the currents originate that can harm the conductors when faults occur. Utility-interactive inverters cannot generate surge currents and usually shut down under conductor fault conditions. Any overcurrent protection should be located at the utility end of the inverter ac output circuit and not at the inverter end of this circuit.

Although the inverter may require an external ac disconnect, if that disconnect function is achieved, as it commonly is, by a circuit breaker mounted at the inverter, then the conductor ampacity calculations may be more complicated as noted below. It is good practice to install the inverter near the backfed load center so that the backfed breaker commonly used to interconnect the inverter with the utility can also be used as the ac inverter equipment disconnect required by 690.15. This places the overcurrent device at the utility-supply end of the circuit and groups the ac disconnect for the inverter with the dc disconnect. An unfused disconnect may be located at the inverter if the inverter must be located some distance from the backfed circuit breaker.

Load-Side Connection

There are two types of connections allowed by the *Code* for interfacing the output of the utility-interactive inverter to the utility power. They are made on either the supply side or the load side of the main service disconnect of a facility or structure (690.64/705.12). The load side of the main service

PHOTO 10.2 Multiple inverters require special connections

disconnect is the most common connection used for the residential system and the smaller commercial system under about 10 kW. *NEC*-2005 Section 690.64(B) [moved to 705.12(D) in 2008 and 2011] covers the requirements and it is heavy reading at best.

Inspectors need to know this material and how to apply it because many PV installers are not familiar with the details of the requirements.

Code-making panels since 1984 have maintained that 690.64(B)(2) will be rigorously applied to any circuits supplied from multiple sources where the circuit is protected by overcurrent protective devices (OCPD) from each source. Such sources would include the output of PV inverter(s) and the utility supply.

This *Code* section requires that the ratings of all OCPD *supplying* power to a conductor or busbar be added together. The sum of the ratings of those breakers must be less than or equal to (in other words: *may not exceed*) 120% of the rating of the busbar or the ampacity of the conductor. In equation form:

PV OCPD + Main OCPD <= 120% R where R is the ampacity of conductor or rating of the busbar.

This equation applies to both residential (dwelling) and commercial installations under both the 2008 and 2011 *Codes*. In the 2005 and previous editions of the *Code*, the 120% allowance was only allowed for dwelling installations and the circuit breaker position requirement discussed below did not exist.

120% factor depends on breaker location

The 120% factor came about in previous code cycles because it was determined that the demand factors on residential and small commercial systems would be such that it was unlikely that the conductor or panel would ever be loaded to 100% of rating. Even if the sources could supply 120% of the rating of the busbar or conductor, loads connected to that same busbar or conductor not exceeding the busbar rating would not pose an overload problem. In order to use this 120% factor, any backfed breaker carrying PV currents must be located at the opposite end of the busbar from the main breaker or main lugs supplying current from the utility (photo 10-1). The same location requirement would apply to the supply (utility and PV) overcurrent devices on any conductor. If the PV inverter OCPD cannot be located as required, then the 120% in the above requirement drops back to 100% and meeting the requirements for the load-side connection becomes more difficult.

The Article 240 tap rules do not apply to these inverter connections since the tap rules were developed only for circuits with one source. The OCPD for the inverter output circuit should be located, as mentioned above, at the point nearest where the utility currents could feed the circuit in the event of a fault.

Examples

1. A dwelling has a 125-amp rated service panel (busbar rating) with a 100-amp main breaker at the top. How large can the backfed PV breaker be assuming that it can be located at the bottom of the panel?

PV OCPD + main OCPD <= 120% of panel rating

120% of panel rating = 1.2 x 125 = 150 amps

PV + 100 <= 150, therefore the PV OCPD can be up to 50 amps

2. Suppose it was 100-amp panel with a 100-amp main breaker. What PV breaker could be added?

PV + 100 <= 1.2 x 100 = 120

The maximum PV backfed circuit breaker would be rated at 20 amps.

3. A 200-amp main panel with a 200-amp main breaker would allow up to 40 amps of PV breaker, which could be any combination of breakers that added up to 40 amps on either line 1 or line 2 of the 120/240-V panel.

PV + 200 <= 1.2 x 200 = 240

PV <= 240-200 = 40 amps

4. When working the problem from the inverter end, we start with the continuous rated inverter output current. This is usually the rated power divided by the nominal line voltage, unless the inverter specifications list a higher continuous output current (sometimes given at a low-line voltage).

A 3500-watt, 240-volt inverter has a rated ac output current of 3500/240 = 14.58 amps.

The output circuit must be sized a 125% of 14.58 = 18.2 amps [690.8(A)(3) and (B)(1)]. The next larger overcurrent device would be a 20-amp OCPD and this would be consistent with the use of 12 AWG conductors if there were not any very large corrections applied for conditions of use or voltage drop. This system could be connected to a 200-amp panel or a 100-amp panel providing the backfed 20-amp breaker could be located at the bottom of the panel (utility input/breaker at the top).

PHOTO 10.3 Utility-required disconnect, fused. Neutral conductor should be passed through and is required on most PV inverters.

There is sometimes a tendency to use that 30-amp breaker and those 10 AWG conductors that happen to be on the truck. While this would pose no problems for conductor ampacity or circuit protection, the inverter specifications may limit the maximum size of the output OCPD and larger values may not be used [110.3(B)].

No bottom breaker position?

From the above equations, it can be seen that if the backfed PV OCPD cannot be located at the bottom of the panel or at the end of the circuit, it is not possible to install the backfed breaker without changing something. That 120% allowance drops to only 100%. Any panel that has a main breaker rated the same as the panel rating in the above equations would not allow *any* OCPD to be added. The 100%-of-the-panel-rating factor (instead of 120%) would equal the rating of the main breaker, and the equation would force the PV breaker rating to be zero.

In a few cases, an *NEC* Chapter 2 load analysis might reveal that the service for the dwelling needed to be only 150 amps, but a 200-amp panel was installed with a 200-amp main breaker just to provide extra circuit breaker positions. In this case, a 150-amp main breaker could be substituted for the 200-amp breaker if the panel is listed for interchangeable main breakers. Even without the bottom position being open, 50 amps of PV breaker could be installed.

Systems with multiple inverters

Many residential and small commercial systems use more than one inverter (photo 10-2). If the local utility requires an accessible, visible-blade, lockable disconnect on the ac output of the PV system, then more than one inverter could not be connected directly to the main panel (photo 10-3). The two, or more, inverters would have to have their outputs combined in a PV ac inverter combining subpanel (PV ac subpanel) before being routed through the utility disconnect, where required, and then to the main panel (photo 10-4). The utility disconnect is not normally fused, but some are, depending on the system configuration. The PV ac subpanel rating, the rating of the disconnect, and the ampacity of the conductor to the main panel are also controlled by 690.64(B)/705.12(D) requirements.

Here is another example.

The dwelling has a 200-amp main service panel with a 200-amp main breaker and there is an empty breaker position (2-poles) at the bottom of the panel. The utility requires an external disconnect switch and it is desired to install a PV system that has a 3500-watt and a 4500-watt inverter. A PV ac panel will be used to combine the outputs of the two inverters and the output of that PV ac panel will be routed through the utility disconnect and then to a single backfed breaker in the main service panel.

Chapter 10 — Load-Side AC Utility Connections

Looking forward to 2014

Inverter Output Circuit Overcurrent Protection. Section 690.9(A) was revised to address current-limited circuits such a PV source circuits and utility-interactive inverter ac outputs. The overcurrent protection for these circuits should be located at the source of the external overcurrents that might damage such circuits.

Load Side Connections. See Appendix H for a detailed discussion of the changes to Section 705.12(D).

The Examples are revised as follows:

1. A dwelling has a 125-amp rated service panel (busbar rating) with a 100-amp main breaker at the top. How large can the PV inverter output (R) be assuming that the backfed PV breaker can be located at the bottom of the panel?

125% R + main OCPD <= 120% of panel rating, Where R is the rated output current of the inverter

120% of panel rating = 1.2 x 125 = 150 amps

1.25R + 100 <= 150, therefore the 1.25R can be up to 50 amps, and R = 50/1.25 = 40 amps

2. Suppose it was 100-amp panel with a 100-amp main breaker. What inverter output could be added?

125% R + 100 <= 1.2 x 100 = 120

The maximum 1.25% R would be at 20 amps. And, the inverter output current rating R would be limited to 20/1.25 = 16 amps

3. A 200-amp main panel with a 200-amp main breaker would allow up to 40 amps of 125% R, which could be 125% of any combination of rated inverter output currents that added up to 40 amps on either line 1 or line 2 of the 120/240V panel.

125% R + 200 <= 1.2 x 200 = 240

The ratings of the output circuits of each inverter are:

3500/240 = 14.58 amps

1.25 x 14.58 = 18.2 amps; use a 20-amp breaker and 12 AWG conductors.

4500/240 = 18.75 amps

1.25 x 18.75 = 23.43 amps; use a 25-amp breaker and 10 AWG conductors.

The 20- and 25-amp breakers are mounted in the bottom of a main-lug-only panel used as a PV ac subpanel. Normally, no loads will be connected to this subpanel. It will be dedicated to the PV system.

The next step is to calculate the backfed breaker that must be placed in the main service panel to handle the combined output of both inverters from the PV ac subpanel and to protect the conductor carrying those combined outputs under fault conditions from high utility currents.

The combined currents from both inverters are:

14.58 + 18.75 = 33.33

and the overcurrent device should be 45 amps (1.25 x 33.3 = 41.7).

The ratings of OCPD's *supplying* the conductor from the PV ac subpanel to the 45-amp breaker, the utility disconnect switch, and the busbar in the PV ac panel are now defined as 45, 20, and 25 amps.

The panel rating and the ampacity of the conductor are controlled by 690.64(B)(2)/705.12(D) and it would be incorrect to guess that the answer might be 45 amps as it would be in a normal load subpanel.

45 + 20 + 25 <= 120% R

PHOTO 10.4 Two inverters with PV ac combining panel. Note neutral conductors.

where R is the panel rating or the ampacity of the conductors.

$$90 \le 1.2\,R, \qquad R \ge 90/1.2 = 75 \text{ amps.}$$

With this number, we would round up to a 100-amp panel, and a 100-amp disconnect would be used. The conductor size for this ampacity would be 4 AWG since the breaker would typically have 75 degree C terminal temperature limits and a 4 AWG conductor can carry up to 85 amps without exceeding the 75 degree terminal temperature limits on the breaker [110.14(C)].

NEC 690.64(B)(2)/705.12(D) is based on worst-case conditions and the requirement to sum the rating of all supply breakers has been in the *Code* since the early days of PV. The requirement assures unconditional conductor or busbar protection, no matter where the supply breakers are placed on the busbar or conductor and no matter where and at what rating any load breakers might be placed on busbar or conductor. This requirement seems to prevent uninformed people from doing uninformed things with respect to adding loads or tapping conductors. Proposals to put conditions and exceptions on this rule to safely allow smaller conductors have been rejected by code-making panels for at least five *Code* cycles, including in the *2011 NEC*. It seems that in some cases, the *NEC* code-making process cannot keep abreast of the requirements for fast-moving, high technology systems. See Appendix E for a technical discussion of this issue.

Summary

The load-side connection for the utility-interactive PV inverter is not the easiest subject to understand, but the correct application of these requirements will yield a safer, more durable system. When the requirements of load-side connections become complex and expensive, a supply-side connection may be used, and we will examine those requirements in the next chapter.

INSPECTORS and PLAN REVIEWERS

PLAN REVIEWERS:
Verify inverter output circuits are sized properly.

Verify 690.64(B)(2)/705.12(D)(2) equations have been applied to all conductors and busbars between the first inverter output overcurrent device and the main overcurrent device at the service disconnect

INSPECTORS:
Verify that backfed PV breakers are located in panels at the opposite end from the utility supply end.

Verify that the conductors used meet plan specifications.

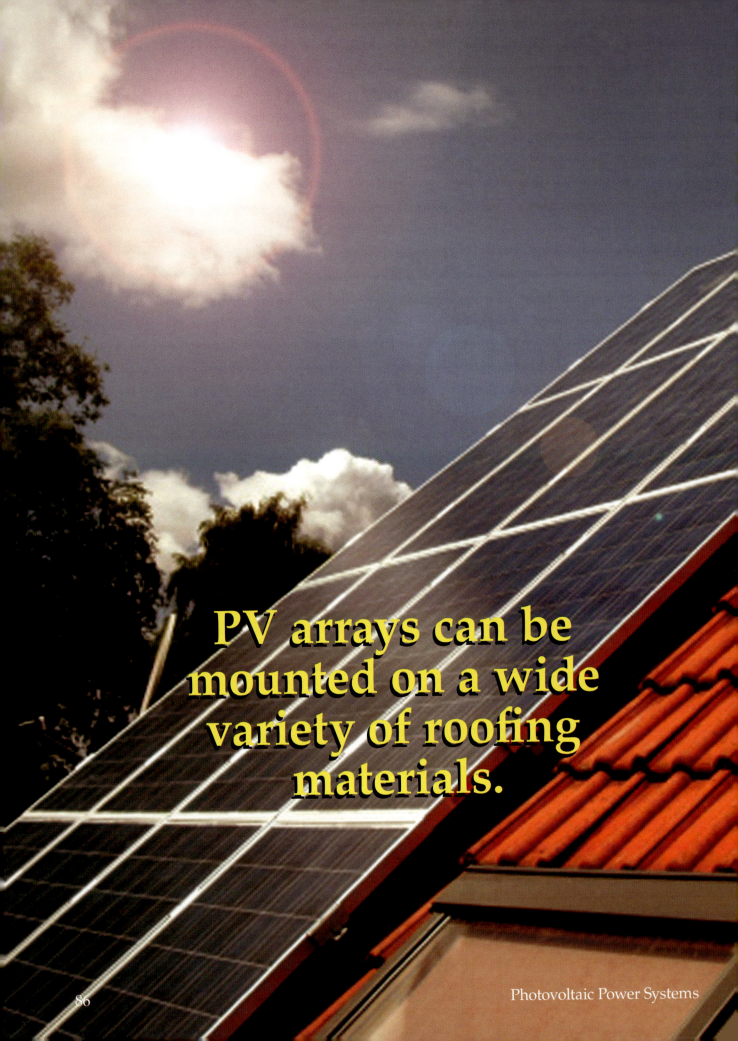

Chapter 11

Supply-Side PV Utility Connections

Many larger PV systems cannot meet the requirements for a load-side (of the service disconnect) connection to the premises wiring system and a supply-side connection must be considered.

Code Considerations

The supply-side connection (also known as a service-entrance connection) is allowed by the *National Electrical Code* and is addressed in a number of sections in the *Code*.

NEC-2011, Section 705.12(A) [690.64(A) in previous editions] allows a supply (utility) side connection as permitted in 230.82(6). Section 230.82(6) indicates that solar photovoltaic equipment is permitted to be connected to the supply-side of the service disconnect.

It is evident that the connection of a utility-interactive PV inverter to the supply-side of a service disconnect is *similar* to connecting a second service-entrance disconnect to the existing service and since these PV conductors are unprotected like service-entrance conductors, many, of the rules for service-entrance equipment *should be considered*. Section 230.2(A)(5)/230.82(6) allows these parallel power production systems as additional services. However, they do not meet the definition of a *service* found in Article 100 of the *NEC*.

Section 240.21(D) allows the service conductors to be tapped and refers to 230.91. In general, the other "Tap Rules" of Section 240 do not apply because they were not developed to address two sources of power in a tap circuit, nor were they developed to assure safe operation when one source is an unprotected utility power source.

Although the PV output is not considered a service, the unprotected conductors are exposed to the same potential fault currents as the service-entrance conductors. It is suggested that this PV connection be as robust as any service entrance. Section 230.91 requires that the service overcurrent device be integral with the service disconnect or located adjacent to it. A circuit breaker or a fused disconnect would meet these requirements (photo 11-1). A utility-accessible, visible break, lockable (open) fused disconnect (aka safety switch) used as the new PV service disconnect may also meet utility requirements for an external PV ac disconnect in areas where utilities require such an additional disconnect (photo 11-2).

Section 230.71 specifies that the service disconnecting means for each set of service-entrance conductors shall be a combination of no more than six switches and sets of circuit breakers mounted in a single enclosure or in a group of enclosures. Section 690.15 allows up to six switches or circuit breakers for the PV *system*, but it is not clear whether these are ac or dc disconnects or both since 690.13 has a similar requirement and appears to be covering dc disconnects only. Common industry practice indicates that an ac disconnect associated with a PV system is not counted against the six allowable disconnects for the existing utility service. This is a gray area subject to AHJ interpretation.

PHOTO 11.1 A breaker as a supply-side tap. But is it *Code* legal?

Location and Directory

Section 230.70(A) establishes the location requirements for the service disconnect. Sections 705.10/690.4/690.54 require that a directory be placed at each inverter and service-equipment location showing the location of all power sources for a building (photo 11-3). Locating the PV ac disconnect adjacent to or near the existing service disconnect may facilitate the installation, inspection, and operation of the system (photo 11-4). Many utilities require the service disconnect and the PV ac disconnect to be co-located.

Size Matters

Obviously the size of the new PV system ac disconnect is important. It will normally be sized at 125% of the rated output current from the PV inverter(s). But in small systems, a question arises; how small can it be? Section 230.79 addresses the rating issue for service disconnects. Some inspectors have looked at 230.79(A) and say that it can be as low as 15 amps if that value is at or above the rating of the inverter output circuit. The connection of other allowed loads at this level is common.

I would suggest caution here, since the connection is to service-entrance conductors rated at 100 amps and above. The typical 15-amp circuit breaker with 10,000 amps of interrupt capability, in this application, may not be able to withstand the available fault current, since it is not protected and coordinated with any main breaker. Of course, Section 110.9 should be followed and available fault current

PHOTO 11.2 Utility-required ac disconnects. Could have been combined into one.

calculated. Also a service-entrance-rated 30-amp fused disconnect with 15-amp fuses could be used.

Another consideration is the size of the service-entrance conductors, the new PV connection conductors, and the size of the terminals on available switchgear rated at 30 or 60 amps. The added conductors between the existing service-entrance conductors and the new PV system ac disconnect will be subjected to available fault currents and will have no overcurrent protection except that provided by the fuse on the primary of the utility distribution transformer. Making them as large as possible, with an upper limit of the size of the existing service-entrance conductors would seem prudent, but small disconnects will not accept very large conductors.

Although these circuits do not meet the definition of service-entrance circuits, the author suggests that Section 230.79(D) be used as the requirement for the smallest PV ac disconnect for PV inverter supply-side connections. Section 230.79(D) requires that the disconnect have a *minimum* rating of 60 amps. This would apply to a service-entrance rated circuit breaker or fused disconnect.

Section 230.42 requires that the service-entrance conductors be sized for the sum of the non-continuous loads plus 125% of the continuous loads. All currents in a PV system are worst-case and are considered to be continuous. The actual rating should be based on 125% of the rated output current for the utility-interactive PV inverter(s) as required by 690.8. The service connection conductors must have a 60-amp minimum rating from 230.79(D). Temperature and conduit fill factors must be applied.

For a small PV system, say a 2500-watt, 240-volt inverter requiring a 15-amp circuit and overcurrent protection, these requirements would appear to require a minimum 60-amp rated disconnect, with 15-amp fuses; fuse adapters would be required. Fifteen-amp conductors could be used between the inverter and the 15-amp fuses in the disconnect, Section 230.42(B) requires that the conductors between the service tap and the disconnect be rated not less than the rating of the disconnect; in this case, 60 amps.

How we would deal with the 60-amp disconnect, 15-amp overcurrent requirements using circuit breakers is not as straightforward. A circuit breaker rated at 60-amps would serve as a disconnect, and

Chapter 11 — Supply-Side PV Utility Connections

PHOTO 11.3 Directory for PV system

it could be connected in series with a 15-amp circuit breaker to meet the inverter overcurrent device requirements. In this case, the requirements of 690.64(B)(2) [705.12(D)(2)] should be applied for the series connection between the two circuit breakers.

Section 110.9 of the *NEC* requires that the interrupt capability of the equipment be equal to the available fault current. The interrupt rating of the new disconnect/overcurrent device should at least equal the interrupt rating of the existing service equipment. The utility service should be investigated to ensure that the available fault currents have not been increased above the rating of the existing equipment. Fused disconnects with RK-5 fuses are available with interrupt ratings up to 200,000 amps.

Section 230.43 allows a number of different service-entrance wiring systems. However, considering that the PV connection conductors are unprotected from faults, it is suggested that the conductors be as short as possible with the new PV service/disconnect mounted adjacent to the connection point. Making these PV feeder connection conductors as large as the service-entrance conductors, while not a *Code* requirement, would also add a degree of safety. Of course, the added disconnect must be able to accept the larger conductors. Conductors installed in rigid metal conduit would provide the highest level of fault protection.

Neutral-to-ground bonding in the ac PV system disconnect is a gray area. Such a bonding may create parallel paths for neutral currents with two adjacent neutral-to-ground bonds and two grounding-electrode conductors to a common grounding electrode, but illustrations in the *NEC Handbook* in Article 250 indicate that these parallel paths do not cause currents that are objectionable. Utility requirements and the location of the PV production or renewable energy credit (REC) meter should be considered.

The actual location of the supply side connection will depend on the configuration and location of the existing service-entrance equipment. The following connection locations have been used on various systems throughout the country.

On the smaller residential and commercial systems, there is sometimes room in the main load center to connect to the service conductors just before they are connected to the existing service disconnect. In other installations, the meter socket has lugs that are listed for two conductors per lug. Of course, adding a new pull box between the meter socket and the service disconnect is always an option.

Combined meter/service disconnects/load centers frequently have significant amounts of interior space where the connection *appears to be possible* between the meter socket and the service disconnect. However, tapping this internal conductor or busbar in a listed device such as a meter-main combination (aka meter-main combo) would violate the listing on the device and should not be done (photo 11-5)

Where the service-entrance conductors are accessible, a new meter base (socket) could be added ahead of the combination device. A connection box would then be added between the new socket and the combination device. The meter would then be moved from the combo device to the new socket, jumper bars added to the old socket and the old socket covered.

In the larger commercial installations, the main service-entrance equipment will frequently have busbars that have provisions for tap conductors. Any holes intended for connections must be marked "Tap Locations" or similar. The PV connection to this tap point can only be made with the approval and instructions from the manufacturer of the equipment or by the organization supplying the service equipment (usually a UL 508 *Industrial Controls Shop*). These organizations can tap the equipment and maintain the listing on the equipment.

In all cases, safe working practices dictate that the utility service be de-energized before any connections are made. Additional requirements in Article 230 and other articles of the *NEC* may apply to this PV feeder connection.

In some locations, a six circuit breaker main-lug-only panel is used as a service-entrance panel. If one of those six circuit breaker positions is unused, it may serve as a supply-side connection for a PV system. The size of the PV inverter output routed through this circuit breaker could be as large as the service-entrance rating or the busbar rating in the load center, whichever is smaller.

After the New PV Supply Side Disconnect

Although 690.64(A)/705.12(A) governs the supply-side connection, as soon as the circuit leaves this

PHOTO 11.4 PV ac disconnect above closed service disconnect

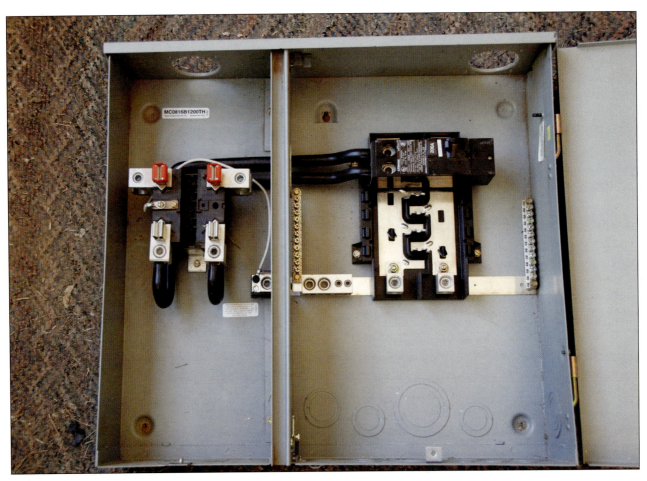

PHOTO 11.5 Meter-main combo—do not tap.

new PV service-entrance disconnect, the requirements of 690.64(B)/705.12(D) apply if there are any overcurrent devices between the service-entrance overcurrent device and any inverter in the system. PV inverter ac combining panels, or load centers needed for multiple inverter installations, and even a circuit breaker in the inverter output circuit serving as a equipment disconnect (690.15) will force the conductor and busbar calculations into 690.64(B)/705.12(D) territory.

One Diagram Is Worth a Thousand Words

Many people do better with diagrams than they do with words, so figure 11-1 should be just up their alley. This big picture diagram can be used with many types of utility interactive PV systems. These systems all start with a meter connected to the utility as shown on the left (blue). After that, we may be dealing with an existing service disconnect and the connected existing load center or with a PV supply-side connection, which is just a second service entrance on the existing premises wiring system. In either case, the *NEC* requirements of Article 230 apply as noted at the bottom of the diagram. In most jurisdictions, the local utility will require a PV disconnect on the ac output of the PV system, and many areas will use a Renewable Energy Credit (REC) meter to measure the PV system output. As shown, one or more single inverters may be connected or even one or more "strings" of microinverters or AC PV modules may be connected to the added combining panel (green blocks). Or, a single inverter could be connected to an existing load center (red blocks). In some cases multiple inverters might be connected through an ac combining panel and then backfeed an existing load center. Let's start our examination of the requirements at the inverter end of the circuit.

Inverter Output Circuit

All utility-interactive inverters have a rated output current that cannot be exceeded. There are no surge currents in these output circuits and *NEC 690.8* requires that the circuit and the overcurrent protective device (OCPD) be rated at 125% of that rated output current. When the calculated OCPD value is a nonstandard value, the next standard higher value should be used, but not to exceed the maximum overcurrent value given in the technical specifications for the inverter. Conductor size should be selected so that it can carry the inverter current and is protected by the OCPD rating.

The asterisk (*) by the 690.8 in the diagram indicates that *if* there is an overcurrent device mounted at the inverter, then the requirements of 690.64(B)/705.12(D), *and not 690.8*, will apply. Some installers and manufacturers use a circuit breaker or fused disconnect at the inverter to meet the requirements of 690.15 to have an equipment disconnect at the inverter. The inclusion of an overcurrent device at this location generally forces the output conductors from the inverter to be larger [as required by 690.64(B)/705.12(D)] than would otherwise required by 690.8.

After the First Inverter Overcurrent Device

Any *conductor or busbar* that can have power flowing from more than one source of supply (under normal or fault conditions) such as the utility and a PV inverter, and where the conductor is protected by an overcurrent device on each supply source must meet 690.64(B)/705.12(D) requirements. This is the longstanding 120% allowance (when 690.64(B)(7)/705.12(D)(7) conditions can be met). Section 690.64(B)/705.12(D) is going to apply to all *conductors and busbars* from the first overcurrent device connected to the inverter output all the way to the service disconnect.

These busbars and conductors would include the busbars of any backfed main panel boards connected to one or two inverters or sets of microinverters, and any busbars in PV ac inverter combiner panels. The conductors or feeders between the panelboards or load centers and the main service disconnects are also subjected to the requirements of 690.64(B)(2)/705.12(D) as noted on the diagram.

In general, the ratings of all of the breakers *supplying* a busbar or conductor are **added** together and the sum is divided by 1.2 (for the 120% allowance). Load breakers are not considered in this calculation. If the location requirements of 690.64(B)(7)/705.12(D)(7) cannot be met (PV breaker located at the opposite end of busbar or conductor from the utility breaker or utility input), then the sum may be divided by only 1, and the busbar rating or cable ampacity goes even higher.

Here is an example. Two inverters each require

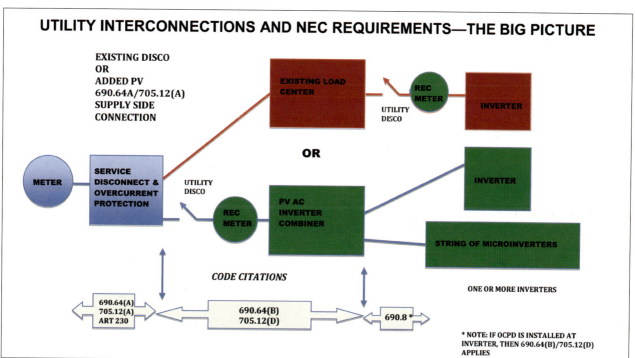

FIGURE 11.1 The Big Picture Diagram

> ### Looking forward to 2014
>
> Section 705.31 now specifies that the overcurrent protection for the supply-side connected PV electric power production source conductors must be located within 3 m (10 ft) of the point of connection to the service conductors. When this overcurrent protection cannot be located within the specified distance, cable limiters or current-limited circuit breakers must be installed at the point of connection in the ungrounded conductors.
>
> With overcurrent protection applied at the PV feeder connection point on the existing service, the requirements for protecting and routing these feeder conductors are no longer as strict as the requirements for unprotected service conductors.
>
> See detailed revisions of Section 705.12(D), Load Side Connections, in Appendix H.

a 50-amp backfed breaker in a main lug PV ac inverter combining load center to meet 690.8 requirements. A supply-side connection is going to be made with a 100-amp fused disconnect. The rating of the combining load center and the ampacity of the conductor to the 100-amp fused disconnect must follow the 690.64(B)(2) requirements.

$$(50 + 50 + 100)/1.2 = 200/1.2 = 166.7 \text{ amps}$$

The numbers indicate that a 200-amp PV ac inverter load center/panelboard would be needed and a 2/0 AWG conductor should be used between that panel and the 100-amp fused disconnect.

Now suppose that the two inverters are being backfed into an existing panelboard (switchgear) and it is not possible to position the two backfed PV breakers at the opposite end of the switchgear busbar from the main breaker. The requirements of 690.64(B)(7)/705.12(D)(7) are not met and the 120% allowance cannot be used. The equation becomes:

(50 + 50 + main breaker) must be less than or equal to the busbar rating.

If the main breaker were rated at 200 amps, then the busbar would have to be rated at 300 amps.

As the diagram shows, 690.64(B) applies to any panel or load center that has connections to the utility and to the PV inverter. It can be an existing load center or an added PV ac inverter combining panel.

The Main Disconnect and on to the Meter

Any circuit between the meter and the service disconnect would be considered a service-entrance circuit and be governed by the requirements of Article 230. However, after passing through the overcurrent device/disconnect on either an existing service disconnect or through the overcurrent device/disconnect on an added PV supply-side connection, the requirements of 690.64(B)/705.12(D) apply all the way to the first overcurrent device connected to the inverter output.

Summary

Supply-side service-entrance connections are useful for larger PV systems where the conditions of the load-side connection cannot be met. These supply-side connections normally require that the power be removed from the service to ensure a safe installation. After the first overcurrent device at the PV service disconnect is passed, load-side requirements may be imposed, depending on the complexity of the system.

The next chapter will address the new micro inverters and ac PV modules.

INSPECTORS and PLAN REVIEWERS

PLAN REVIEWERS:

Verify that 690.64(A)/705.12(A) and 690.64(B)/ 705.12(D) have been properly applied to size the disconnects, overcurrent devices, and conductors.

INSPECTORS:

Verify that the PV disconnect has been installed correctly with line-side terminals toward the utility and that appropriate bonding and grounding have been accomplished.

An ancient way and modern way to capture solar energy

Photovoltaic Power Systems

Chapter 12

The Microinverter, The AC Module and DC-To-DC Converters

No discussion of PV systems would be complete without a look at the newest inverter technologies that the installer and inspector will face. These new technologies include the microinverter and the AC PV module as well as dc-to-dc converters.

Microinverters

The inverters that have been covered in previous chapters are known as "string inverters" because they operate with a string of series-connected PV modules. These inverters range in power from more than one megawatt down to about 700 watts. DC maximum system voltages range from 125 volts to 1000 volts and higher.

The Enphase microinverter is a typical example (photos 12-1 and 12-2); it is a small inverter (hence the name) that is designed to work with a single PV module and to operate at a maximum of about 70 volts on the dc input. The inverter is connected directly to the PV module using the existing conductors and connectors (now locking in most cases) attached to both the module and the inverter. Available units are rated in the 170–215 watt range, but as with other PV products, ratings and specifications change continually.

The microinverter is a utility-interactive inverter and must have dc ground-fault protection [690.5 or 690.35(C)] per the requirements of UL 1741 just as required in the larger inverters. The Enphase microinverter has been on the market since early 2009 and it internally grounds the positive dc module conductor. That internal grounding bond (via the dc ground-fault protection circuits — *NEC* 690.5) requires that the inverter have a dc grounding electrode terminal and that the terminal is on the out-

PHOTO 12.1 Enphase 215 W microinverter   Courtesy Enphase

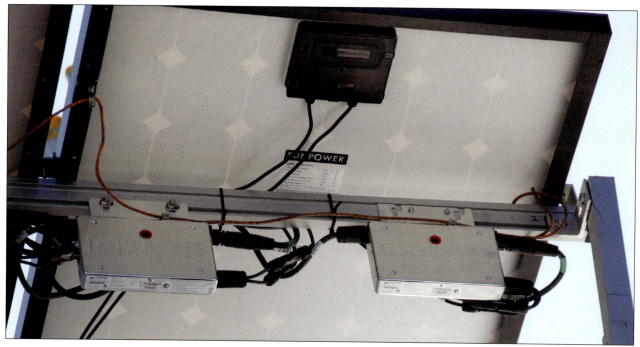

PHOTO 12.2 Pair of Enphase microinverters showing ac and dc cables

side of the Enphase microinverter case. This single terminal serves as both the dc grounding electrode terminal and the ac and dc equipment grounding conductor terminals for the inverter. Other types and brands of microinverters may accomplish grounding differently or go to an ungrounded configuration using modules with the new "PV Cable" required by *NEC* 690.35 for such systems.

The microinverter has ac input and output cables and connectors and has been listed in a manner that will allow multiple inverters to be connected with up to about 15 units on a single output cable (photo 12-3). The dc and ac connectors used with the Enphase microinverter have been listed as load break rated disconnects. With a power output in the 170–215 watt range (depending on model), the rated ac output current at 240 volts will range from 0.71 amps to 0.9 amps. On the 14 AWG cable with a 15-amp overcurrent device, the rated continuous current for that circuit is limited to a maximum of 12 amps. This rating will allow 1–15 inverters to be installed on the same ac output cable.

Proper Grounding Is Somewhat Complex

Enphase elected not to put an ac equipment-grounding conductor in the four-wire ac output cable and connector assembly on the M190 microinverter. That cable assembly has 240-volt line 1, line 2, and neutral conductors. The fourth conductor is reserved for the three-phase version of this device. The installer must consider the lack of that ac equipment grounding conductor in the ac output cable.

NEC requirements dictate that systems with microinverters (and any PV system with inverters mounted near the modules) have dc equipment grounding conductors for the modules and any rack (690.43), ac equipment grounding conductors for the inverter outputs (250.110), dc inverter grounding electrode conductors [690.47(C)], and even module/array grounding electrode conductors for ground-mounted installations [690.47(D)-2008 *NEC*].

There are probably several ways of meeting these various grounding requirements under any *Code* edition including 2005, 2008 and 2011. One method is as follows:

Use a 6 AWG bare copper conductor running continuously through all inverter "grounding" lugs and then directly to the existing ac grounding electrode for the ac premises wiring. This meets 690.47(C) dc grounding electrode conductor (GEC) requirements for the inverters if the existing grounding electrode is a ground rod. A concrete-encased electrode (UFER) might require a bare copper grounding electrode conductor not larger than

Chapter 12 — The Microinverter, The AC PV Module and DC-To-DC Converters

PHOTO 12.3 Microinverter AC output connector

4 AWG, but conductor sizes would generally allow a 6–8 AWG GEC (250.166).

If a 14 AWG tap were made to this GEC near the last inverter output cable and connected to a bare or green conductor in the ac conduit or cable leading to the premises load center, then the requirements for the inverter ac equipment grounding conductor (EGC) would also be met.

And, if that bare 6 AWG conductor were to be continued past the inverters and connected to each module frame and any rack metal surfaces, both the dc EGC and the array dc grounding electrode conductors would be met [690.43 and 690.47(D)].

AC PV Modules

Take a normal dc PV module *in the factory* and connect a microinverter to it, fasten the microinverter to the back of the module and cover the *dc*, exposed conductors so none of them are accessible and you have an AC PV module (photo 12-4). AC PV modules are coming to the market. One is the AC PV module by Westinghouse Solar and it has a unique frame that is also the module mounting rack. Photo 12-5 shows a Canadian Solar AC PV module with concealed dc conductors. Since the dc wiring between the module and inverter is no longer accessible and has become an integral part of the product, dc requirements in the *Code* no longer apply to the AC PV module. The AC PV module is a utility-interactive device and has a similar ac output cabling system to the microinverter addressed above.

DC Connections

In the standard PV module/microinverter combination, the microinverter dc connection to the PV module may have to be disconnected to replace the microinverter should it or the module fail (say once in every 20–30 years). While the voltage will be a maximum of about 70 volts with current inverter designs, the current may be in 3–7 amp range and the connectors could possibly be damaged at this voltage and current, posing a possible safety hazard. While a very few inspectors may request a costly and impractical load-break-rated disconnect, the code-compliant solution is really quite simple. The back of the PV module must be accessed to reach these dc connections and this generally requires that the module be unfastened from the mounting system. Since the module is accessible and *is* being accessed, just putting a blanket or other opaque material over it per 690.18 will reduce the dc output voltage and current (and the ac current) to near zero, allowing the module/inverter dc connectors to be safely opened. Opening this connection with the module blacked out will, in all likelihood, be safer than opening the same connectors on a module in a high-voltage string of modules. Of course, the AC PV module has no accessible dc connections, and the AC PV module will have no accessible dc disconnects.

AC Connections

Each microinverter or AC PV module will have an ac input/output cable to allow the multiple inverter parallel connections. This cable may carry currents in bright sunlight of 0.875 amps at 240 volts (current designs) from the first module/inverter in the set to as much as 12 amps at 240 volts through the last connector of the set that has multiple series-connected devices. Servicing the single AC PV module or utility-interactive microinverter could be accomplished by covering the module to reduce the

PHOTO 12.4 Almost an AC PV Module. Just make the dc wiring not accessible.

dc and, hence, the ac current to zero. However, not covering all modules in the set would allow current from other, non-covered, modules/inverter to flow through the cable and at 240 volts, could damage the connector and possibly pose a shock hazard when opening these ac connections under load. To some extent, the hazard is minimized because the inverter anti-islanding circuits shut down very rapidly, reducing any arcing when the ac connector is opened.

Opening the ac circuit at the PV backfed breaker in the building service-entrance panel would be a safe solution if that breaker could be locked open, but breaker locks are few and far between and lockout/tag-out procedures are not generally used in residential and commercial electrical systems.

NEC Section 690.14(D) addresses the situation and it would appear that the installation of a separate ac disconnect on the roof near the AC PV Modules or microinverters will meet *Code* requirements and enhance safety. A common 60-amp unfused, pullout, air-conditioning disconnect costs less than $10 at the building supply centers. It provides the disconnect, a place to terminate the ac output cable from a set of microinverters or AC PV modules, a place to originate the field-installed wiring system to the ac load center in the house, and is usually cheaper than a separate junction box and cover.

Some microinverters and AC PV modules may have dc and ac connectors fully listed as load-break-rated disconnects. The Enphase microinverter has both the ac and dc connectors listed as load-break-rated disconnects. Such a rating would meet *NEC* 690.14(D) and 690.15 disconnecting means requirements and the separate roof top disconnect would not be required, although the device mentioned above would still be an inexpensive transition point between the inverter/module ac cord and the conduit conductors leading from the roof.

Advantages Will Boost the Market

The use of microinverters and AC PV modules will proliferate due to several advantages they offer over the conventional string inverters.

The first is a simplified set of installation requirements and a reduced number of separate parts. See photos 12-6 and 12-7 for some quantitative differences in the amount and types of equipment

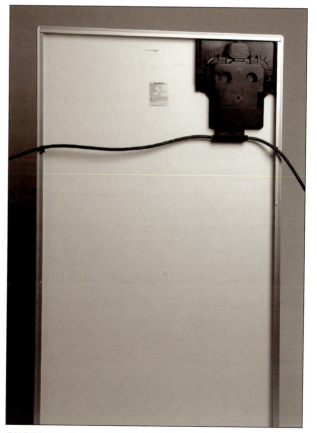

PHOTO 12.5 Back of AC PV Module as defined in 690.2 and 690.6 *Courtesy Canadian Solar*

Chapter 12 — The Microinverter, The AC PV Module and DC-To-DC Converters

Looking forward to 2014

Section 690.47(D) has been returned to the *Code* and may affect microinverter systems.

AC PV Modules. The various certifying/listing Nationally Recognized Testing Laboratories (UL, ETL, TUV, CSA) are listing module/microinverter assembled combinations with exposed dc conductors and connectors as AC PV modules so the requirement for concealed dc conductors and connectors used to previously define an ac PV module no longer applies. The question that then remains, do the dc connector requirements apply and it appears probably not because of the wording in Section 690.6 that excepts the AC PV Module from all dc source circuit requirements in the *Code*.

Some instruction manuals for AC PV modules prohibit separating the microinverter from the PV module should repairs to the microinverter be necessary. Other manuals from different manufacturers give detailed instructions for performing such separation and for returning only the microinverter for repair. Future revisions to UL 1741 should clarify the definition of an AC PV module and the requirements for allowing field modification of the assembled unit.

AC AFCI now required. Section 705.12(D)(6) now requires that the microinverters that have exposed wire harnesses or exposed ac output cables have an ac arc-fault circuit interrupter (AFCI) on that circuit if it operates at 240 volts, 30 amps or less.

DC-to-DC Converters. Section 690.8(A)(5) now requires that the maximum current for dc-to-dc converters connected to the PV module output be the rated continuous current for such devices. Of course, many of these devices interact with the PV inverter and this number may vary with the array configuration.

In 2014, dc-to-dc converters will begin appearing inside module junction boxes and the entire device will be listed as a single piece of equipment. Close attention to the installation instructions for the "active" PV module will be required. In many cases, the standard module voltage and current requirements found in sections 690.7, 690.8 and 690.9 may not apply. Again section 110.3 will be the driver; and plan reviewers and inspectors must require that instruction manuals be included in the permit packages; and they must become familiar with these instructions and devices.

involved in installing an AC PV module system vs. a conventional string inverter system.

In a dc series-connected string of PV modules, module mismatch is sometimes an issue that affects the string performance. Modules come out of the factory, with slight (up to 10%) variations in performance. The string of modules in a dc system cannot deliver current above the current delivered by weakest module in the string. The mismatch between module currents results in some lost power compared to a dc string of modules that are equal in every specification. The PV modules near the top of an array on a sloped roof may operate hotter than modules lower down on the roof due to hot air rising behind the modules. Depending on how each string of modules is connected, some loss of power may occur if hot modules are connected in series with cooler modules.

Shading is also a problem in a conventional string-inverter configuration. The shading of a single module will result in a power loss from that module, but may also reduce power from the other, non-shaded modules in the string.

The microinverter and the AC PV module work at the individual module level. Each inverter extracts the maximum power from that module no matter what the other modules in the PV array are doing. The output of each is independent of the other modules/inverters in the set. The outputs of the microinverters or AC PV modules are connected in parallel, rather than in series, and this isolates one from another.

The outputs are at 120 and 240 volts ac and these ac output circuits act much like ac branch circuits. They go dead when the ac utility power is removed at any disconnect in the circuit so they

PHOTO 12.6 Numerous parts are required for a string inverter system PV.

longevity of about 15 years. The microinverter manufacturers, using different construction methods and topologies, are predicting significantly longer lives for their products. Time will reveal all.

A Word of Warning

The microinverter or AC PV module output must be connected on a dedicated circuit per 690.64(B)/705.12(D). See the previous chapters in this book for details on how to connect multiple sets of these devices. They should never be connected to a circuit protected by a GFCI or AFCI because neither of these devices has been tested or listed for backfeeding.

DC-to-DC Converters

DC-to-dc converters are on the market and are small boxes with leads that attach to the output of each module. These boxes act somewhat like a microinverter by decoupling the actions of one module from others in the string so that shading is less of a problem. Of course, the output of these devices is dc, not ac like the microinverter, and they come in several variations. Some of these devices can be used on just a few modules in a PV array, but others

do not pose the safety hazards associated with the daytime "always-energized" dc circuits operating at hundreds of volts between the modules and the inverter. If a short circuit or ground fault were to occur in these ac output circuits, the dedicated branch-circuit breaker would open and the circuit would go dead. Opening the main service disconnect or the backfed PV breaker will de-energize those PV ac output circuits — a boon to fire fighters.

Disadvantages

There may be some cost impact of using AC PV modules or microinverters on each module when compared to the use of the single string inverter. However, two factors must be considered. The cost of the dc switchgear and the required conduit (or other appropriate wiring method) for the dc conductors inside the building plus the cost of the single inverter must be compared to the added cost of multiple small inverters or AC PV modules with an inverter on each module.

Then there are the life cycle costs. Modules are guaranteed for power production for 25 years, but can be expected to produce power for as long as 50 years. Large inverters generally have an average

PHOTO 12.7 Far fewer parts are needed to install the Andalay PV/microinverter system

Chapter 12 — The Microinverter, The AC PV Module and DC-To-DC Converters

are required for every module. Some devices work with a standard string inverter, but others require a special inverter. Most are connected in series like a normal string used with a string inverter. A few others are required to be connected in parallel.

In some cases, the specialized inverter required with some of these devices communicates and controls the performance of the individual dc-to-dc converters connected to each module. Removing the ac power from the inverter or turning it off, can, in some cases, shut down the individual converters, removing dc voltages from the wiring.

These devices are not addressed in even the *2011 NEC* because of the wide variation in system design and connection requirements. The requirements of Section 690.72(C) [*NEC* 2011] may have some bearing on the connection of these devices. However, since all of these dc-to-dc converters should be listed, the installers and the inspectors are generally going to have to rely on the instruction manuals and labeling supplied with these new devices for proper system design and installation. The concepts of short-circuit current and open-circuit voltages used in the design and installation of standard string module systems will not apply to these products.

Summary

Numerous microinverters and AC PV modules are being installed and while they are directed at the smaller residential systems, systems as large as several megawatts have been installed using microinverters. They are being sold in the home improvement centers and building supply houses as well as in local electrical supply houses and the general public is buying them. Inspectors must become familiar with these devices and the *Code* requirements that apply to them.

INSPECTORS and PLAN REVIEWERS

PLAN REVIEWERS:
Verify whether the installation uses microinverters or true AC PV Modules. The ac output circuits must meet *NEC* requirements for the utility interface (690.46(B)/705.12(D). A second, readily accessible ac disconnect must appear on the plans. This may be provided by the utility disconnect, where required.

INSPECTORS:
Verify that grounding and disconnect requirements are met. Rooftop inspections appear necessary. In jurisdictions where AHJs are not permitted to be on roofs due to insurance requirements, it appears that the only way an inspection may be partially accomplished is by reviewing a good photographic record provided by the installer of all of the necessary code-required details.

Chapter 13

PLAN CHECKING AND INSPECTING

PV systems are a relatively mature technology that is rapidly moving into common usage in the residential and commercial arenas. Unfortunately, these systems are not just common electrical load systems that are supplied by the utility and that have remained relatively unchanged for decades. They represent a distributed power system that not only supplies power to local loads, but also sends excess power to the utility distribution network. These PV systems also have a very long life and will be producing dangerous voltages and currents for decades. Inspecting these systems will take more time and effort than inspecting the typical electrical system. Starting with a good plan check will facilitate the on-site inspection.

PV PLAN CHECK

Electrical inspectors and electrical permitting personnel are seeing increasing numbers of photo-

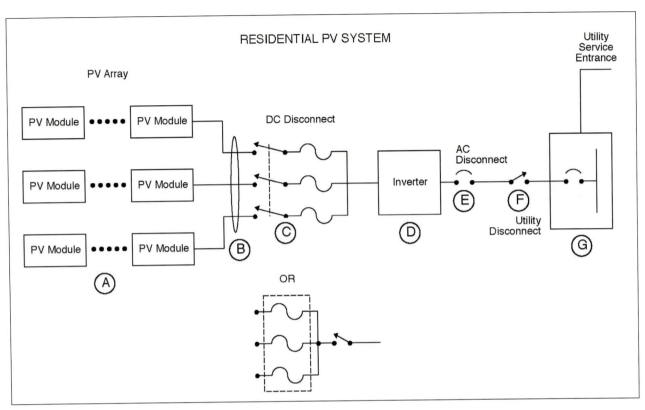

FIGURE 13.1 One-line PV system diagram

voltaic (PV) power systems, both at the permitting stage and at the initial inspection. Both processes go much more smoothly for all concerned when the electrical system is properly documented. Since the typical PV installer has not installed hundreds of the same PV system, and the inspector has not seen hundreds of these systems, the documentation for these systems must, by necessity, be somewhat more detailed than the documentation associated with a typical residential electrical system. This chapter will examine a typical *residential*, utility-interactive PV system in terms of a package that should be submitted by the installer when applying for a permit or discussing the system with the plan reviewer or the inspector prior to installation. Commercial systems are similar, but can be more extensive and involve higher voltages at the ac utility interface and in the dc voltages from the PV array.

Equipment Lists and Specifications

A list of the equipment used and the specifications for that equipment should be included with the permit. This list would include the PV-specific equipment such as the PV modules, the inverter, the fuses, and circuit breakers. Listing/certification and rating information must be included. The specifications of this equipment are necessary to determine if the conductors have been properly sized and that the fuses and circuit breakers used in the dc parts and ac parts of the system are properly rated. Factory cut sheets or pages from instruction manuals are the preferred way to present this information.

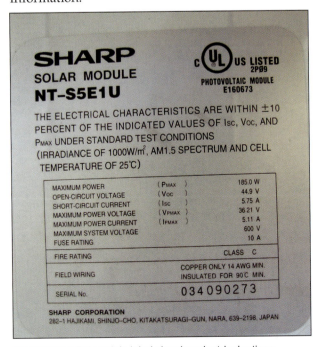

PHOTO 13.1 PV module label showing electrical ratings

104

Photovoltaic Power Systems

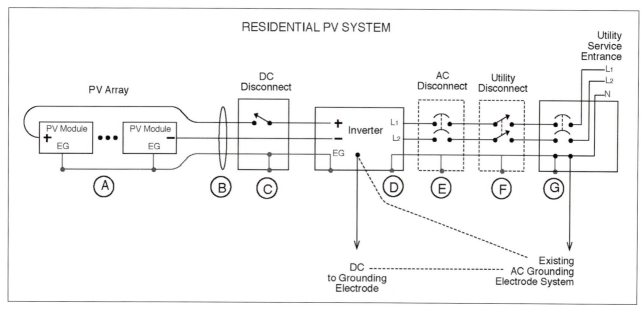

FIGURE 13.2 Three-line PV system diagram

Since the PV modules and inverters are constantly changing, the preferred option would be to include copies of the installation manuals for the inverter, module, and dc PV combiner with each submission. Since not all module installation manuals include the technical specification, the technical specifications should also be included.

The Diagram

A one-line diagram such as shown in figure 13-1 should accompany the permit application. Actually, since the details of disconnects and grounding are not familiar to all involved, a three-line diagram would be even better as shown in figure 13-2. While a formal CAD-generated diagram on 24" x 36" paper is not required, something better than a "back of the envelope" sketch should be presented. The circled letters in the figures will be referenced below to indicate information that should appear on or be attached to the plan.

The System

On the one- and three-line diagrams, the following information should be indicated, or that information should be attached.

A. PV Array

A.1. The type and number of PV modules in each series string should be indicated. The open-circuit voltage (Voc) of each module, times the number of modules connected in series, times a cold temperature factor (690.7) equals the maximum systems voltage and must be less than the maximum direct current (dc) input voltage of the inverter and less than the voltage rating of connected direct-current (dc) equipment (wires, overcurrent devices, disconnects). The coldest expected ambient temperature should be noted on the diagram. A label on the back of each module as shown in photo 13-1 will give the electrical parameters needed for the code-required calculations. These values should appear on the diagram. A photo of the label should be included since this label will not be visible once the modules have been installed.

A.2. The ampacity of module interconnection cables, not less than the larger of: 1.56 times the module I_{sc} or conditions of use applied to 1.25 I_{sc}. Due to the exposed, outdoor location and high operating temperatures, all conductors should have insulation rated for 90°C and wet conditions (in conduit, THHN/THWN-2, XHHW-2 or RHW-2). Exposed conductors (usually USE-2 or PV Cable/PV Wire) must be suitable for the hot, wet, outdoor environment.

B. Conduits

B.1. Conduits will typically be used throughout the system and specifically after the dc wiring leaves the PV array and runs through the structure. They will be installed in various locations, some of which may be in sunlight. See 310.15(B)(2)[310.15(B)(3)] for temperature adders. The average high and

Chapter 13 — Plan Checking and Inspecting

PHOTO 13.2 DC PV disconnect with required markings

the height of the conduit above the roof should be specified. Conduit fill and conductor ampacity calculations for conduit fill and temperature calculations should be included or attached.

One source of temperature correction factors for conduits in sunlight is Copper Development's web site:

http://www.copper.org/applications/electrical/building/pdf/rooftop.pdf

B.2. The PV source circuit or PV output conductors must remain outside the structure until they reach the readily accessible PV dc disconnect unless the conductors are installed in a metallic raceway [690.14, 690.31(E)]. The exception for the use of metal conduits inside the building does not apply to the ac output of utility-interactive inverters since these circuits are similar to ac branch circuits.

C. Module and String Overcurrent Protection and PV DC Disconnect

C.1. Overcurrent protective devices (OCPD) in dc circuits may not be required when there are only one or two strings of modules connected in parallel to the inverter. Three or more strings of modules typically require an OCPD in each string. The current rating of the OCPD, when required, should be 1.56 Isc for that circuit (690.8, 690.9). The voltage rating of the OCPD should be not less than the maximum PV systems voltage found in A.1. The strings may be combined in parallel in a combiner box ahead of an unfused dc PV disconnect or combined at the output of the dc PV disconnect (figure 13-1 and photo 13-2). See Appendix F for a more detailed look at the calculations and the requirements for OCPD in the dc PV array circuits. Any OCPD connected in series with a module or string of modules should not have a value greater than the maximum series fuse value marked on the back of the module (photo 13-1).

C.2. The PV array output should be connected to the top or line side of the main dc PV disconnect. The circuit from the dc PV disconnect to the inverter dc input should be connected to the bottom or load side of the disconnect. The grounded PV output conductor (usually the negative conductor) must not be switched by the disconnect, and this grounded conductor must be color-coded white. Some recent PV systems have a positive conductor that is the grounded conductor; it will be color-coded white, it will not be switched, and in this case, the ungrounded negative conductor will be connected to the switch pole. PV systems may not have any grounded PV array circuit conductors when used with non-isolated, transformerless inverters and then both PV output conductors would be switched and neither would be color-coded white (690.35).

C.3. PV output conductors, after any combining

PHOTO 13.3 Inverter with internal ac and dc disconnects

of series strings, should have an ampacity of not less than the larger of: 1.56 times the module I_{sc} times the number of strings in parallel *or* conditions of use applied to 1.25 I_{sc} times the number of strings in parallel. The overcurrent device must always protect the conductors. Additional details on sizing conductors and overcurrent devices will be found in Appendix D.

D. The Inverter

D.1. The inverter must be listed for utility-interactive (U-I) use (690.60).

D.2. The inverter maximum input voltage must not be exceeded in cold weather (110.3(B)). See A.1.

D.3. Most PV systems must have a 690.5/690.35 dc ground-fault protection device (GFPD). When a GFPD is built in to the inverter (nearly all U-I inverters), there should be no external (to the inverter) bond between the grounded circuit conductor and the grounding system. Additionally, an equipment grounding conductor must be routed from the PV array through the dc PV disconnect all the way to the inverter.

D.4. In addition to ac and dc equipment grounding conductors, the inverter must also have a provision for a dc grounding electrode conductor when used with a grounded PV array, and that conductor must be properly connected to the grounding system (690.47). This requirement is found in 690.47(C) and many U-I PV systems meet the dc grounding requirements by using the various methods described in Chapter 9. The dotted lines in figure 13-2 show alternate routing and bonding for the dc grounding electrode conductors.

D.5. AC and/or dc disconnects internal to the inverter are acceptable if the inverter is readily accessible and the AHJ judges that only qualified people will service the inverter (photo 13-3). Otherwise, external disconnects will be needed (photo 13-4). Internal disconnects, if circuit breakers, will not protect the ac output circuits from utility-sourced

PHOTO 13.4 Inverter with external ac and dc disconnects

Chapter 13 — Plan Checking and Inspecting

PHOTO 13.5 Inverter ac disconnect combined with the utility disconnect to the right of the inverter

fault currents and an external OCPD will be needed at the utility point of connection.

E. Inverter AC Output Overcurrent Device and Disconnect

E.1. Any OCPD located in the inverter ac output should be rated at 1.25 times the rated continuous output current of the inverter. The rated continuous current is specified in the inverter manual or is calculated by dividing the inverter rated output power by the nominal ac line voltage. This OCPD may be a backfed breaker located in the dwelling load center, the place where any possible fault currents for the inverter ac output conductor would originate. A backfed breaker in the dwelling load center could also be the inverter ac disconnect (690.15) if the inverter were located near the load center.

E.2. The inverter ac disconnect should be "grouped" with the dc inverter disconnect and both should be "near" the inverter. The AHJ determines the definitions of "grouped" and "near." Most systems use the PV disconnect (see B.2.) as the dc inverter disconnect, but if the PV dc disconnect is on the outside of the building and the inverter is on the inside, a second dc inverter disconnect may be required inside the building at the inverter location. The same thing would apply if the backfed circuit breaker in the building load center were on the outside wall and the inverter were on the inside. A disconnect (usually a circuit breaker) would be required inside the building near the inverter.

E.3. From the above, it becomes obvious that the system diagram should show the physical location of all components.

F. Utility-Required AC Disconnect

F.1. Many utilities require a visible-blade, lockable-open disconnect in the ac output circuit of the inverter. This disconnect is usually located within sight of the service-entrance meter so that emergency response people can easily find it. The top termi-

Looking forward to 2014

Marking and Labels. The requirements for marking PV circuits and placing warning labels on PV circuits have been increasing with every code cycle.

Requirements for reflective red backgrounds with white letters 9.5 mm (3/8 in) high are found in several sections where Warning Labels are required. See 690.31 (G)(3) and (4) and 690.56(A) and (C). Where other labels are required in Article 690 and throughout the *Code*, Section 110.21(B) is referenced which requires that such labels have effective words/colors/symbols. An Informational Note refers to ANSI Z535.4-2011, Product Safety Signs and Labels.

Increasing Equipment Complexity. As described in Chapter 1, new equipment coming to the market is evolving more rapidly than the *Code* is able to keep up with. It becomes increasingly important for the instruction manuals of listed equipment like inverters, charge controllers, AC PV modules and dc-to-dc converters be included in the permit package. Only in this way, can the plan reviewer and the inspector keep apprised of the required installation requirements for the newer equipment.

nals (line side) of this disconnect should be connected to the circuit that comes from the utility [supply side connections, 690.64(A)/705.12(A)] or the ac load center [load side connection, 690.64(B)/705.12(D)] since it will usually be energized by utility voltage. The bottom terminals (load side) should be connected to the circuit from the inverter. This disconnect may be fused or unfused depending on the specific requirements of the utility. Photo 13-5 shows an ac disconnect to the right of the inverter that serves as both the ac inverter disconnect and the utility-required ac PV system disconnect. The utility point of connection is inside the house through a backfed circuit breaker in the load center.

F.2. The utility disconnect must have a minimum current rating of 1.25 times the maximum continuous output current of the inverter (690.8).

G. Point of Connection-Load Center

G.1. Most of the smaller residential and commercial PV systems will make the point of connection with the utility through a backfed breaker in the building. *NEC* Section 690.64(B)/705.12(D) establishes the requirements. A 120% factor is allowed if the backfed PV breaker is located at the opposite end on the panel from the utility-fed main breaker or main lugs. If the load center is rated at 100 amps and has a 100-amp main breaker, the maximum current from all backfed PV breakers would be 20 amps (either or both phases of the 120/240 panel). A 200-amp load center with a 200-amp main breaker would be limited to 40 amps of backfed breakers. However, many installations have PV systems that are larger than the 100-amp or 200-amp load centers can accommodate. In these cases, other load side connections are possible as is a supply-side connection to the service-entrance conductors.

Summary

All of the above information should be included in plans submitted for obtaining a permit for the installation of a PV system. The more information submitted, the easier it will be for the PV system designer/installer to communicate to the inspector/permitting official that the system design and component selection meet the requirements of the *NEC*. It is far more cost effective to change the design on paper before any hardware is purchased and installed than it would be after the system has been installed. Ready for the inspection? Read on.

INSPECTORS and PLAN REVIEWERS

PLAN REVIEWERS:
This is your chapter

See Appendix G for more detailed checklist

INSPECTORS:
Encourage your jurisdiction to hire well-qualified plan reviewers.

Chapter 13 — Plan Checking and Inspecting

Hal Kissinger Retired Chief
New Mexico Inspector and John Wiles

Chapter 14

THE 15 MINUTE PV INSPECTION
CAN YOU? SHOULD YOU?

In some jurisdictions, inspectors have as little as 15 minutes to make a residential electrical inspection. A common question is, "Can I inspect a residential PV system in 15 minutes?" This chapter will examine that question and also take up the question, "Should only 15 minutes be allocated for inspecting a residential PV system?"

Let's start with an ideal situation. The inspector is familiar with PV systems in general and has inspected quite a few. He or she receives an application for a permit for a PV system, and that application is accompanied by all of the material outlined in the preceding chapters in this book. A plan review of the supplied material shows no major problems in code-compliance, and the installer quickly rectifies the few minor problem areas found. A team consisting of a PV vendor with a history of good PV installations and an electrical contractor/electrician who has a commercial electrical license and some PV experience has done the design of the system and the installation.

Here are some of the items that an inspector should verify during the site visit. They are listed in order of importance and in order of safety for the inspector. For a more complete list, see the Inspector/installer Checklist found in Appendix G.

Grounding

Proper grounding of the PV system is extremely important because the PV modules will be generating hazardous amounts of energy for the next fifty years or more. Proper grounding is the first, the last, and the most important area (in the author's experience) that requires code-compliance in a PV system. Proper grounding of all exposed metal surfaces that may become energized as the system ages or as accidents happen will provide the highest levels of protection against shock and fires. Proper grounding will also facilitate the action of the ground-fault protection and arc-fault protection equipment that these systems will have. As the inspector moves through the PV system, grounding will be a critical inspection item in several locations.

Many smaller PV systems (below 10–20 kW) may have all of the PV equipment, both ac and dc, grounded by a single "grounding" conductor connected from the modules to the grounding bus bar in the existing ac load center. The module frames, the PV array mounting rack, and the dc disconnect are connected with a dc equipment grounding conductor that connects to the inverter. From the inverter through one or more ac disconnects, a combined ac equipment grounding conductor/dc grounding electrode conductor continues the connection to the ground bus bar in the ac load center [690.47(C)]. This grounding method permitted by 690.47(C) is only one possible grounding method and the permissive methods of 690.47(C) in the 2005 *NEC* may also be used and found on many PV systems. The 2011 *NEC* combines and clarifies the 2005 and 2008 *NEC* 690.47(C).

The first item an inspector should verify is that the ac equipment grounding conductor from the PV system inverter has been connected properly in the ac load center grounding bus bar and that the ac load center has a proper connection to ground (earthed). If this equipment grounding *has not* been done properly, a ground fault in the PV array or

PHOTO 14.1 Improperly wired 240-volt inverter; neutral wired to PE terminal

elsewhere in the system may put several hundred volts (with respect to the ground where the AHJ is standing) on the ungrounded exposed metal surfaces of any PV equipment.

As PV systems mature and UL standards and the *Code* evolve, it is hoped that the grounding of PV systems will become more robust. Even now under 2005 through 2011 *Codes*, many systems will be installed with a dc grounding electrode conductor connected to a dc grounding electrode or to the ac grounding electrode.

AC Point of Connection to the Utility

While the residential ac load center is open to check the grounding connection, the location and value of the backfed PV circuit breaker can be noted. It should match the value on the permit application and shall not be greater than 20% of the load center rating. It should be located at the opposite end of the busbar from the utility input. This assumes that the main breaker and the load center have the same rating. See *NEC* 690.64(B) [705.12(D) in 2011 NEC]. This requirement limits the backfed PV breaker to a maximum of 20-amps on a 100-amp load center and to a

> ## Looking forward to 2014
>
> **Grounding.** The return of Section 690.47(D) to the *Code* requires the direct grounding of the PV array module frames and racks to a grounding electrode in addition to the equipment grounding conductors.
>
> **PV circuits and the Rapid Shutdown Requirement.** New equipment may be required to meet the requirements of Section 690.12. Multiple strings from the PV array to the inverter may be replaced by a combiner at the array with a remotely controlled contactor disconnect inside. Inverters may require an external disconnect remotely operated to reduce dc input terminal voltage rapidly. Systems with batteries, may require shunt trip (remote-controlled) circuit breakers between the batteries and the inverters to meet the requirement. Unfortunately, this new equipment and the need to inspect it will slow down the inspection process.

PHOTO 14.2 Inverter with three dc inputs

maximum of 40 amps on a 200-amp panel. Breakers larger than this indicate that the utility connection should have been made on the supply side of the service disconnect. *See chapters 10 and 11 for more details.*

Inverters

The inverter should be opened to check the field-installed connections. Some inverters will require metric hex socket drivers (or Allen wrenches) to open. One manufacturer makes a sealed inverter with permanently attached cables for connections to the adjacent ac and dc disconnects.

Inverters with a 120-volt output should have line (ungrounded), neutral (grounded), and equipment grounding conductors between the load center and the inverter. Inverters made outside the U.S. may have the equipment grounding terminals marked PE for "protective earth." Some 240-volt inverters have only line 1, line 2, and equipment grounding conductors with no neutral (grounded) conductor, while others will have line 1, line 2, neutral, and equipment grounding conductors. The inverter manual (submitted with the permit request) will show the proper connections. Inverters requiring no neutral connection must not have the neutral terminal in the utility circuit attached to anything, particularly an equipment grounding terminal, because such a connection would make a double bond between ground and the neutral conductor that is prohibited by *NEC* Section 250.6 (photo 14-1).

The dc input connections to the inverter may include one or more sets of positive and negative conductors as well as at least one dc equipment grounding conductor routed to either an external dc disconnect or to the PV array (photo 14-2).

AC and DC Disconnects

Each disconnect should be properly grounded with the equipment grounding conductors or metal raceways. Following and verifying the equipment grounding conductors backwards from the ac load center through the system to the PV modules is important to ensure that each exposed metal surface that may be energized is grounded. Grounding using sheet metal screws is prohibited by the *Code* and the use of thread cutting screws and aluminum lugs is questionable (photo 14-3). Most listed fused disconnects and circuit breaker enclosures have ground-bar kits with specific mounting instructions and locations that should be used to maintain the listings of the devices and to provide the highest quality grounding connection (photo 14-4). Metal conduits with dc circuits operating over 250 volts will usually require grounding/bonding bushings (250.97).

While the dc PV disconnect enclosure is opened, the color coding of the conductors should be checked. Most current PV systems use a negative ground and the negative conductor should be colored white and should *not* be switched or fused by the disconnect.

PHOTO 14.3 Improperly grounded dc disconnect

PHOTO 14.4 Properly installed, listed ground-bar kit

There are also positive grounded PV systems being installed, and in this case, the positive conductor is now colored white and is not switched. Section 690.35 permits the use of ungrounded systems (neither of the circuit conductors is grounded) and these will become more common. These ungrounded systems must meet several additional requirements including switching both of the ungrounded circuit conductors with neither conductor colored white. See *NEC* 690.35. The inverter or the system should be clearly marked (not yet a *Code* requirement) showing the type of grounding (negative ground, positive ground, or ungrounded) to allow easy determination of the proper color codes.

There is no specified color code for the ungrounded conductors, and any color is permitted as long as gray, white, green, and green and yellow are not used. Figure 14-1 shows the typical conductor insulations that may be seen.

Both circuit conductors (positive and negative) should be routed through the disconnect enclosure even though only the ungrounded conductor is switched. Avoiding a "switch loop" configuration ensures that both circuit conductors are always in close proximity for best functioning of overcurrent devices and to allow a bolted connection point for the grounded conductor on an isolated "neutral bus" in the enclosure, if required.

In the "switch-type" dc PV disconnect, the always "hot" conductors from the PV array wiring should be connected to the top (covered) "Line," terminals on the switch while the lower, exposed, "Load" terminals should be connected to the inverter. On the ac disconnect, the upper "Line" terminals should be connected to the utility power conductors that come from the backfed ac load center or a supply-side utility connection. The lower "Load" terminals should be connected to the inverter.

Workmanship and the Roof

The equipment used and the workmanship on most residential PV systems will more closely resemble the equipment and workmanship on a commercial electrical installation than those items in a residential electrical system. There will usually be surface-mounted disconnects and much of the wiring will be in exposed, surface-mounted conduit.

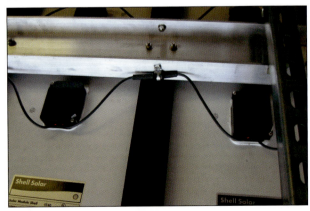

PHOTO 14.5 Module wiring properly secured

Photovoltaic Power Systems

System Type	Negative Conductor	Positive Conductor
Negative Ground	White or Gray *	Black or Red
Positive Ground	Black	White or Gray *
Ungrounded	Black	Red

*Code Requirement, others optional

Typical DC Wiring Conductor Colors

FIGURE 14.1 Typical DC Wiring Conductor Colors

PHOTO 14.6 A 40 kW PV system-safe now. Still safe in 40 years? Courtesy Solectria.

Chapter 14 — The 15 Minute PV Inspection — Can You? Should You?

The installer should have a ladder on-site the day of the inspection to facilitate examining the installed PV array. A quick look at the PV array on the roof should verify that any exposed wiring is firmly secured to the PV modules or the mounting structure and is not dangling down where it would be subject to physical damage (photo 14-5).

If the backs of the PV modules can be closely observed, proper grounding of the modules should be checked. The hardware supplied by the module manufacturer should have been used as shown in the instruction manual delivered with the permit application. Each PV module must be grounded, and if exposed, single-conductor cables touch the mounting racks or a metal roof, those objects should also be grounded. See chapter 4 for more details on module grounding.

The conductors used for module interconnections should be as specified in the permit application with respect to size (AWG), insulation type, and temperature rating. Any PV combiners containing overcurrent devices exposed to sunlight should be noted and the plans and technical data reviewed to determine if adequate temperature deratings were applied. Conduits in sunlight will also be exposed to higher-than-ambient temperatures.

Inspect in 15 Minutes?

Yes, it *might* be possible to perform the above inspections in 15 minutes if the inspector has spent some time at the plan-check stage and is experienced in PV systems employing this inverter and the installer is there to answer questions, open the inverter and other equipment as necessary and to provide a ladder for roof access. However, any problems found in the above areas should warrant a closer look at the entire system and when more details are examined, the inspection time can grow. A lack of familiarity with either PV in general, the equipment being installed, or the installer would normally dictate that the inspection take more time. How much? Some residential PV inspections for new inspectors are somewhat of a training session and with a knowledgeable installer, examining and discussing all of the details relating to a durable, safe (for 50-years) installation might take two or more hours.

Should We Do 15-Minute Inspections?

See the little girl in photo 14-6? That PV system she is touching will still be producing power when her grandchildren are her age. It *will* take more than a 15-minute inspection to ensure that the PV system will be as safe then as it is now. Fifteen minutes is probably insufficient time to ensure the public safety of a system that will operate over a 40–50 year period.

INSPECTORS and PLAN REVIEWERS

PLAN REVIEWERS:

Do your finest work to ensure that the PV system is code-compliant on paper and ready for inspection.

Don't approve any PV system permit application with less than 100% code-compliance.

INSPECTORS:

Be safe and ensure the safety of the public.

APPENDICES

Appendix A — PV Math

Appendix A
PV Math

As we look at the PV array in a PV system, we find that many installers and inspectors are confused by the new system voltage calculations that may be required by the *Code* specific to PV systems. *Code* Fine Print Notes (FPN) [changed to Informational Notes in *NEC*-2011] also address voltage drop that may be applied to the dc wiring from the array to the inverter. This article will cover both of those subjects.

PV Math—Module Open-Circuit Voltage

A PV module or a string of series-connected modules has a rated open-circuit voltage (V_{oc}) that is measured (and labeled on the module) at an irradiance of 1000W/m^2 and a cell temperature of 25 degrees Celsius (C) (77 degrees Fahrenheit (F)). This voltage increases from the rated voltage as the temperature drops below 25°C. It is necessary to calculate this voltage at the expected lowest temperature at the installation location to ensure that it is less than the maximum input voltage of the inverter *and* less than the voltage rating of any connected cables, switchgear, and overcurrent devices (usually 600 volts). Since parallel connections of strings do not affect the open-circuit voltage, the number of strings connected in parallel is not involved with this calculation.

Where module temperature coefficients are available, Section 690.7 (starting in the 2008 *NEC*) requires that the open-circuit voltage (V_{oc}) of a PV array be determined at the lowest expected temperature at the installation location. In previous editions of the *NEC*, Table 690.7 could be used to determine a multiplier that was applied to either the module or string (series connection of PV modules) rated V_{oc}. The table can also be used under the *2008 NEC* where module temperature coefficient data are not available.

The rated V_{oc} is measured at 25°C (77°F) and is printed on the back of the module and in the technical literature of the module. To use the table, all one has to do is to determine the lowest expected temperature, look up the factor from the Table for that temperature (which ranges between 1.02 at 24°C to 1.25 at -40°C), and multiply the factor by the rated V_{oc}. Note that in the 2011 *Code*, the table has a finer breakout of temperature for better resolution than the 2008 *Code*.

For example, a module has a V_{oc} of 35 volts and is going to be installed where the temperature dips to -17°C. The factor from Table 690.7 in the *2008 NEC* is 1.18 and the cold temperature V_{oc} for this module is 35 x 1.18 = 41.3 volts.

If 12 modules were going to be connected in series, the string V_{oc} in cold weather would be 12 x 41.3 = 495.6 volts.

We could also calculate the string voltage at rated conditions first and then apply the temperature factor. In this case, the 12 modules in series would have a string open-circuit voltage of 12 x 35 = 420 volts at 25 degrees C. Then we apply the 1.18 factor and get 1.18 x 420 = 495.6 volts; the same answer as before.

While the table is still valid and has been refined with 5°C increments in the 2011 *Code*, new modules may have different technologies than the silicon module technology used to develop the table.

2008 NEC Requirements Differ

Table 690.7 is based on an average type of crystalline PV module that has been the most widely used over the last 30 years. However, we now have modules with different internal types of PV cells, and the table may not apply very well to these newer modules. Section 690.7 in the *2008 NEC* requires that where the module manufacturer's temperature coefficients data are available they will be used. These temperature coefficients are found in the technical literature of nearly all modules and can also be obtained directly from the manufacturer. Unfortunately, different manufacturers present the temperature coefficients in two different forms.

Percentage Coefficients

One way of presenting these data is to specify them as a percentage change, and they are expressed as a percentage change in V_{oc} for a *change* in temperature measured in degrees C. Note that the temperature used is a *change* in temperature from the rated 25°C.

For example: The V_{oc} temperature coefficient is given as

-0.36% per deg C   or   -0.36% / °C.

The module has a V_{oc} of 45 volts at 25°C (77°F) and is going to be installed where the expected lowest temperature is -10°C (14°F). Because the temperature coefficient is given in degrees C, we must work in degrees C. The *change* in temperature is from 25°C to -10°C. This represents a change in temperature of 35 degrees. The minus sign in the coefficient can be ignored as long as we remember that the voltage *increases* as the temperature goes *down* and visa versa. Of course, if you are an engineer or a mathematician, feel free to use the minus sign in an algebraic equation.

If we apply the coefficient, we can see that the percentage change in V_{oc} resulting from this temperature change is

0.36% / °C x 35°C = 12.6%.

This percentage change can now be applied to the rated V_{oc} of 45 volts. And, at -10°C, the V_{oc} will be 1.126 x 45 = 50.67V.

Eleven of these modules could be connected in series and the cold-weather voltage would be 11 x 50.67 = 557.37V, and that voltage is less than a 600-volt equipment limitation.

Millivolt Coefficients

Other PV module manufacturers express the V_{oc} temperature coefficient as a millivolt coefficient. A millivolt is one, one-thousandth of a volt or 0.001V.

A typical module with an open-circuit voltage (at 25°C) of 65 volts might have a temperature coefficient expressed as

-240 mV per degree C or -240 mV/°C

If we install it where the expected low temperature is -30°C (-22°F), then we have a 55°C degree change in the temperature from 25°C to -30°C. Again, we must work in degrees Celsius, since that is the way the coefficient is presented.

Millivolts are converted to volts by dividing the millivolt number by 1000.

240 mV / 1000 mV/V = 0.24 volts

The module V_{oc} will increase 0.24 V/°C x 55 °C = 13.2 volts as the temperature changes from 25°C to -30°C.

The module V_{oc} will increase from 65 volts at 25°C to 65 + 13.2 = 78.2 volts at the -30°C temperature.

Let us suppose that the inverter maximum input voltage was listed as 550 volts. How many modules could be connected in series and not exceed this voltage? We take that maximum inverter voltage of 550 volts and divide it by the cold-weather open-circuit voltage for the module of 78.2 volts.

550 / 78.2 = 7.03 modules and the correct answer   would be seven (7) modules.

7 x 78.2V = 547.4V

Eight modules could not be used because the open-circuit, cold-weather voltage would exceed 550 volts.

8 x 78.2V = 625.6V

Expected Lowest Temperature?

Where do we get the expected lowest temperature? Normally, this temperature occurs in the very early morning hours just before sunrise on cold winter mornings. The PV modules are, in many cases, a few degrees colder than the air temperature due to night-sky radiation effects. The illumination at dawn and dusk are sufficient to produce high V_{oc}, even when the sun is not shining directly on the PV array and has not produced any solar heating of the modules. And in many locations, cold temperatures are coupled with high winds and the winds remove any solar heating from the module, even in bright sun.

A conservative approach would get weather data that show the record low temperatures and use this as the expected low temperature. Other data show more moderate low temperatures associated with the data used to size heating systems. See the Informational Note on 690.7 in the *2011 NEC*. The National Renewable Energy Laboratory (NREL) maintains data on a web site that shows the record lows for many locations in the U.S.

http://rredc.nrel.gov/solar/old_data/nsrdb/1961-1990/redbook/mon2/state.html

Local airports and weather stations may have historical data on low temperatures

Also, weather.com has some of these data on file accessed by zip codes:

http://www.weather.com/weather/climatology/monthly/zip code

PV Math—Module Short-Circuit Current

In most silicon PV modules, the module short-circuit current does increase very slightly as temperature increases, but the increase is so small as to be negligible at normal module operating temperatures. It is normally ignored.

Fine Print (Informational) Notes—Voltage Drop

Fine Print Notes [now Informational Notes] are not part of the *Code*—at least until the AHJ reads them, and then they become part of his or her personal code.

In the common, utility-interactive PV system, the PV array may operate at a nominal 48 volts to voltages near 600 volts. With nominal, peak-power, and open-circuit voltages to deal with, the installer and inspector are sometimes in a quandary as to how to calculate the voltage drop from the PV array to the inverter.

The utility-interactive inverter will normally operate in a manner that keeps the array voltage near the peak-power voltage (also called the maximum power point). While this voltage can vary with temperature, and temperatures vary considerably, using the rated maximum power point voltage

and maximum power point current of the modules results the easiest method of calculating voltage drop.

A typical PV array may have a single string of ten modules in series connected to the inverter 200 feet away with 10 AWG USE-2/RHW-2 conductors. The maximum power point numbers for the module are:

$V_{mp} = 45V$ $I_{mp} = 5.5$ amps, where the subscript mp means at maximum power.

For a single string of 10 modules, the string maximum power point numbers are:

$V_{mp} = 450V$ $I_{mp} = 5.5$ amps.

Table 8 in Chapter 9 of the *NEC* gives conductor resistance per 1000 feet at 75°C.

For an uncoated, stranded 10 AWG conductor, the resistance is 1.24 ohms per 1000 feet.

The total conductor length (both ways) must be used in the calculation and this is 400 feet.

The resistance for 400 feet of a 10 AWG conductor is $400/1000 \times 1.24 = 0.496$ ohms.

The current at the maximum power point is 5.5 amps. Voltage drop is found by multiplying this current by the conductor resistance:

$5.5 \times 0.496 = 2.728$ volts.

Expressed as a percentage, $2.278/450 \times 100 = 0.606\%$ or about 0.6% and that is much less than the IN recommendation of three percent for most circuits. Of course, the losses in the PV dc disconnect were not counted, but they are typically less than one percent on these circuits.

Voltage Drop — Another Perspective

When dealing with the dc input circuits of a utility-interactive inverter, the inverter operates the array at the maximum power point with a maximum power voltage (V_{mp}) and a maximum power current (I_{mp}). Since these parameters are affected by irradiance and temperature, it is difficult to determine what voltage and current should be used in the voltage drop equation. The procedure above uses the module specifications at Standard Test

Conditions that are based on the rating conditions of an irradiance of 1000W/m² and a cell temperature of 25°C (not a very realistic temperature under actual operating conditions). One conservative approach is to use the module manufacturer's specified normal cell operating temperature (NCOT) from the module data when it is available. NCOT is typically in the range of 42 to 52°C and is a measured temperature of the module when the irradiance is 800W/m², ambient temperature is 20°C and the wind is blowing across the module at 1m/sec. This temperature is used to adjust the Vmp and Imp numbers presented at Standard Test Conditions (STC) to values associated with the higher NCOT. Vmp will be reduced and Imp increased very little if at all. Voltage drop will be reduced.

Appendix B

Connecting and Wiring Microinverters and AC PV Modules

See Chapter 12 for an overview of microinverters and AC PV modules. Due to unclear definitions in the UL standards and in the *Code*, it is not possible to determine if combinations of PV modules and microinverters combined/assembled in the field or at the dealer or distributor meet the intent, definition, or requirements associated with true AC PV Modules as defined in 690.2 and in 690.6.

As of early 2014 there is no specific size associated with either microinverters or AC PV modules. The power outputs are increasing with nearly every new product.

Instructions supplied with this listed product should be followed [*NEC* 110.3(B)]. The suggestions below do not substitute for compliance with the *NEC*, local codes, or the instruction manual for listed products.

Microinverters and AC PV modules have similar ac output characteristics, connections and code requirements.

Grounding

Both the AC PV module and the microinverter will require equipment-grounding connections where there is any exposed metal in these devices. A grounding electrode connection will be required when the microinverter operates the module in a grounded manner.

Equipment/Safety grounding
The ac output circuit cable of some microinverters does not have an ac equipment-grounding conductor (EGC). This EGC conductor must be started (originated) in the transition box on the roof where each set of inverters has the final factory ac output cable (aka trunk cable) connected to another wiring system. This ac EGC must be routed to the nearest equipment grounding conductor in the existing premises wiring as it would be in any other ac circuit. There is no requirement that it be unspliced and the size will typically be 14 AWG per Table 250.122.

System/Functional grounding
True AC PV modules where there are no readily accessible dc conductors or dc disconnect will normally not require a grounding electrode conductor or terminal for such a conductor. Since both the requirements in the *2005 NEC* 690.47(C) and the "permitted" requirements 690.47(C) in the *2008 NEC* are both based on Article 250, the provisions of either editions of the *Code* appear to be applicable in jurisdictions using either edition. *NEC* 690.47(C) in

the 2011 *NEC* combined and clarified 2005 and 2008 *Code* requirements in this area.

Under UL Standard 1741, the microinverter, if it isolates the dc grounded input conductor (assuming one output conductor of the module is internally grounded in the microinverter) from the ac output, must have a dc grounding electrode conductor running from the grounding electrode terminal on the microinverter case to a dc grounding electrode. If the microinverter operates the PV module as an ungrounded system (neither positive or negative connected to ground), then no grounding electrode conductor would be required.

Section 690.47(C) in the *2008 NEC* appears to *permit* the use of a combined ac EGC and dc grounding electrode conductor (GEC) from the inverter. In the *2011 NEC* 690.47(C)(3), the requirement is clear. UL 1741 requires the dc GEC terminal on the outside of the inverter. If this option is elected, then the 8AWG minimum (250.166) grounding electrode conductor from each inverter must be bonded to the input and output of each metal conduit and metal box that it travels through until it gets to the main grounding bar in the service entrance equipment or to the first grounding bar origination a grounding electrode conductor to a grounding electrode. The bonding requirement and 8 AWG size would appear to rule out the use of 10-3 with ground type NM cable for the ac output circuit. The bonding requirement may also be cumbersome to implement multiple times and the routing of this combined conductor may induce lightning surges to enter the main load center and other branch circuits. The permissive method of grounding described in 690.47(C) in the *2008 NEC* may also be used under the *2005 NEC*.

Alternatively, the permissive grounding method described in the *2005 NEC* 690.47 may also be used under the *2008 NEC* as an alternative to the *2008 NEC* 690.47. Section 690.47(C) in the *2005 NEC* and 690.47(C) in the *2008 NEC* are based on the general requirements of Article 250.

Section 690.47(C) in the *2011 NEC* combines and clarifies the grounding methods described in the 2005 and *2008 NEC*.

The Exception in 690.47(D) in the *2008 NEC* regarding array grounding is not clear. The subject of the section refers to Array Grounding Electrodes. It is not clear if the Exception removes the requirement for an additional array grounding electrode only and leaves the requirement for the array GEC or removes the requirement for both. The intent of the submittal was to use a new array GEC to ground the array to an existing electrode. This would be particularly important in a high lightning area, but that is a performance issue, not a safety issue. This section was not in the *2005 NEC* and was removed from the *2011 NEC*.

The size of the dc grounding electrode conductor is determined by 250.166 and this section has been clarified in the *2008 NEC*. In many cases, but not all, a 6 AWG bare copper conductor will meet the requirements. Where a UFER (concrete-encased electrode) is used, a 4 AWG grounding electrode conductor will usually be required. A short 6 AWG conductor may have to be irreversibly spliced to the 4 AWG conductor at each microinverter and connected to the microinverter grounding terminal if the inverter grounding terminal will not accept a 4 AWG conductor directly. An alternative would be to drive a single ground rod six or more feet from the UFER ground, ground the inverters and modules as described below with a 6 AWG bare copper grounding-electrode conductor and then bond the ground rod to the UFER with a 4 AWG bonding jumper (690.47C(1) in *2005 and* 2011 *NEC*)

The dc grounding electrode conductor may terminate at the service entrance grounding electrode or at a grounding electrode associated with any subpanel where the inverter dedicated circuits end in backfed breakers under the *2005 NEC*. Under the *2008 NEC*, the combined conductor dc GEC/ac EGC can be terminated at the main service grounding bus bar or at any subpanel bus bar that has a grounding electrode attached and where the inverter backfed breaker terminates. The *2011 NEC* allows either location to be used.

Disconnects

The microinverters should be installed in compliance with 690.14(D) of the *NEC*. As noted in this section, there are requirements for dc and ac disconnects on the roof in this not-readily accessible area, and an additional ac disconnect in a readily accessible location.

The relatively low dc voltage (usually less than 70 volts) and currents (less than 8 amps) may allow the dc connectors on the microinverter inverter to serve as the dc disconnects for servicing the inverter. However, if the dc connectors are opened under load, the resulting arc *may* damage the connectors and possibly pose a shock hazard. This is especially true when these connectors are used on modules in a high voltage (up to 600 volts) string of modules connected to a typical string inverter. The module can easily be covered with an opaque material to reduce ac and dc currents to zero. In a similar manner, the ac connectors on the microinverters and AC PV modules could be used as the maintenance disconnects required by 690.15.

Microinverter and AC PV Module manufacturers can have the ac and dc connectors designed and listed *with* the microinverter or AC PV module as load break rated disconnects and this will allow the use of these connectors to meet *Code* requirements (690.14, 690.15 and 690.17).

Even with load break rated ac connectors, a transition box is needed to change from the flexible ac output cable to the *Code*-required fixed wiring system that will enter the building. An inexpensive unfused 60-amp 240-volt air conditioning pull out disconnect would serve nicely and is already in a NEMA 3 R enclosure. It will also serve as an ac disconnect that when pulled, will shut down the microinverters or AC PV modules and opening the ac circuit will reduce the dc currents to very near zero in those dc connectors allowing safer opening of the dc disconnects.

Such a disconnect can also be used to meet some AHJ requirements for a non-connector disconnecting means on the roof.

690.14(D)(3) requires an additional disconnect and that disconnect requirement may be met by the backfed breaker in the load center where the load center is positioned to meet the accessibility and location requirements of 690.14(C)(1). Some jurisdictions are requiring that this second ac disconnect be on the outside of the building and any utility-required disconnect on the inverter output circuit would usually meet this requirement.

AC Output Circuits

The output circuit of any utility-interactive inverter up to the first overcurrent protection device (OCPD) is very much like an ac branch circuit. If the utility voltage is removed from this circuit (for any reason), the circuit becomes de-energized (dead)--just like a branch circuit. If there is a line-to-line or line-to-ground fault on this circuit, the OCPD responds in a normal manner to the fault currents generated by the utility. The inverter(s) can generate no more than its rated current per UL Standard 1741 and when the fault occurs, the drop in line voltage will normally cause the inverter to shut down. And when the branch circuit breaker opens in response to the fault, the inverter shuts down.

It would appear that these inverter output circuits could be wired using any Chapter 3 wiring method suitable for the environment (hot, wet and UV outside and hot in attics). Grounding requirements or methods used for microinverters may dictate conductor sizes too large for 10 AWG type NM conductors.

An AC GFCI device *should not* be used to protect the dedicated circuit to the microinverter or AC PV module even though it is an outside circuit. None of the small GFCI devices (5 ma-30 ma) are designed for back feeding and will be damaged if backfed. In a similar manner, most AC AFCIs have not been evaluated for backfeeding and may be damaged if backfed with the output of a PV inverter.

Combing multiple sets of microinverters or AC PV modules

In multiple strings of these inverters, there is no *NEC* requirement that an ac combining panel (load center) be located on the roof. In fact, most NEMA 3R load centers must be mounted against a surface to keep water from penetrating holes in the back panel. Such a surface may have to be added in order to properly mount a 3R load center on the roof. And then there might be problems meeting 110.26 clearance requirements. A further issue with OCPD on the roof is heating of the device over its rated 40 degrees C operating temperature. Gray load centers in the sun will normally operate 10-20 degrees C hotter than the ambient temperature. This may be difficult to compensate for when considering available equipment, the size of the ac conductors attached to the inverters, and listing restrictions on the inverters. Never the less, it is possible to mount an ac load center on the roof with proper solar shielding and use it to combine the outputs of U-I inverters or sets of microinverters.

The rating of any combining panel and the ampacity of conductor from that panel to the backfed breaker in the main load center as well as the rating of the main load center and the backfed breaker must meet 690.64(B)/705.12(D) requirements. This requirement will require a combining panel and conductor with a rating nearly twice sum of all of the 15-amp or 20-amp backfed breakers used for each output. See the 120% allowance in 690.64(B)(2)/705.12(D)(2) and 690.64(B)(7)/705.12(D)(7).

The ac output conductor for a set of inverters must have an ampacity of 125% of the continuous currents for all of the inverters on that circuit. The backfed circuit breaker in the panel must be rated the same and if an odd current rating is determined, the breaker rating should be the next larger size. The breaker must protect the conductor under the conditions of use and the conductor ampacity must be derated for those conditions of use.

The ac output circuit from each set of inverters must have an equipment-grounding conductor to facilitate OCPD operation during ac ground faults. Some microinverters have a three-wire output through a four-contact connector. The unused terminal in the connector is reserved for future use. The three active pins in the connector are 240V L1 and L2, and a neutral. There is no ac equipment-grounding conductor. This lack on an equipment-grounding conductor in the cable requires that the equipment-grounding conductor for the microinverter or AC PV module be an external connection to the inverter case, where the case is metal. This external equipment-grounding conductor must be connected to the fixed wiring system (usually, but not always conduit) where that wiring system originates.

Unless the microinverter bracket has been designed and evaluated as a grounding/bonding jumper, grounding the microinverters does not ground the rack or the modules and visa versa.

There is only one ac neutral-to-ground bond in an ac electrical system. That bond is made in the existing service entrance equipment. No additional neutral-to-ground bonds should be made when installing a PV system unless a supply-side service entrance connection is made or transformer isolation establishes a separately derived system.

AC PV Module Grounding— A Gray Area

Combinations of a microinverter and a PV module with exposed dc connectors and dc conductors between the PV module and the microinverter are being certified/listed as AC PV modules. Some of these products have instruction manuals that say the microinverter *may not* be removed from the PV

Looking forward to 2014

Grounding. Section 690.47(D) has been returned to the *Code* after being absent in the 2011 *NEC*. It has been revised for clarity and will apply to a PV array using microinverters or AC PV modules. The array fames or structure will be connected directly to a grounding electrode with a grounding electrode conductor sized per 250.166. If the premises wiring system grounding electrode is in close proximity (within 1.8 m (6ft)) to the location selected for the array GEC dropping the earth, then the premises grounding electrode may be used.

Disconnects. In the 2014 *NEC*, Section 690.14 was removed. The requirements in this section were merged and revised with the requirements previously found in 690.13 and 690.15. There are no significant changes with respect to the requirements for microinverters and AC PV modules.

AC Output Circuits. All microinverters and AC PV modules have an exposed, flexible cable for the ac output circuit and usually for the trunk cable connecting a set of these devices. Section 705.12(D)(6) requires an ac AFCI on this output circuit if it is rated at 240 V and 30 amps or less. *Note:* Many of the available backfed AFCI breakers have not been listed nor should they be used as a backfed breaker.

See the revised requirements for load centers being used for inverter or microinverter ac combining panels in 705.12(D) and as elaborated on in Appendix H.

The definition of the AC PV module has not been clarified in the *NEC* nor in the UL Standards as of January 2014.

module. Other manuals give specific instructions for removing the microinverter from the PV module for repair. At issue is the definition of an AC PV module as a factory assembled unit and the potential need to meet all dc *Code* requirements for these products with exposed dc connectors and dc conductors. Section 690.6 exempts the AC PV module from dc wiring *Code* requirements. However, exposed connectors are subject to loosening or being opened in the field. Connectors and conductors are exposed to environmental degradation, ground faults and arc faults, and animal damage.

Also at issue is the microinverter-to-PV module frame bonding when the mechanical/electrical connection is broken in the field. When the microinverter is replaced, how is the bonding connection quality verified and how is the certification/listing maintained without NRTL evaluation?

At some point, these issues will be addressed in UL Standard 1741 and possibly in the *National Electrical Code*.

Appendix C

Grounding PV Modules

Grounding PV modules to reduce or eliminate shock and fire hazards is necessary but difficult. Copper conductors are typically used for electrical connections, and the module frames are generally aluminum. It is well known that copper and aluminum do not mix as was discovered from numerous fires in houses wired with aluminum wiring in the 1970s and dissimilar metals are not to come into contact with each other (110.14). PV modules generally have aluminum frames. Many are anodized for color or have mill finishes, and many are clear coated. The mill finish aluminum and any aluminum surface that is scratched quickly oxidizes. This oxidation and any clear coat or anodizing form an insulating surface that makes for difficult long-lasting, low-resistance electrical connections (e.g., frame grounding). The oxidation/anodizing is not a good enough insulator to prevent electrical shocks, but it is good enough to make good electrical connections difficult.

Underwriters Laboratories (UL) Standard 1703 (developed by UL and maintained by the Standards Technical Panel (STP) 1703) is used to certify and list all PV modules sold in the U.S. and requires very stringent mechanical and electrical connections between the various pieces of the module frame to ensure that these frame pieces remain mechanically and electrically connected over the life of the module. These low-resistance connections are required because a failure of the insulating materials in the module could allow the frame to become energized at up to 600 volts (depending on the system design). The *National Electrical Code* (*NEC*) requires that any exposed metal surface be grounded if it could be energized (250.4 and 250.110). The installer of a PV system is required to ground each module frame (690.43). The Code (110.3(B)) and UL Standard 1703 require that the module frame be grounded at the point where a designated grounding provision has been made. The connection must be made with the hardware provided (if any) using the instructions supplied by the module manufacturer.

The designated point marked on the module must be used since this is the only point tested and evaluated by the certification/listing agency for use as a long-term grounding point. Underwriters Laboratories (UL) has established that using other points such as the module structural mounting holes, coupled with typical field installation "techniques," *may not* result in low-resistance, durable connections to aluminum module frames. If each and every possible combination of nut, bolt, lock washer, and star washer could be evaluated for electrical properties and installation torque requirements, *and* if the installers would all use these components and install them according to the torque requirements, it might be possible to use the structural mounting holes for grounding.

New grounding devices are coming to market that will eventually ease the problems of module grounding, but until they have been evaluated with specific modules and the module instructions address these devices, they do not meet the requirements of UL Standard 1703 or *NEC* Section 110.3(B).

Some U.S. PV module manufacturers are providing acceptable grounding hardware and instructions. Other manufacturers are frequently providing less-than-adequate or no hardware and unclear instructions. Future revisions of UL 1703 should address these issues. In every case, the module manufacturer's hardware and instructions should be used (where possible) to ground the module at the points marked on the frame. After August 2007,

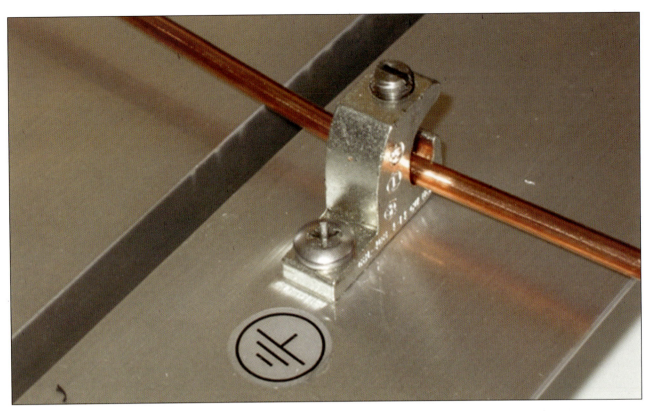

PHOTO 1 Lay-in lug

UL Standard 1703 required that the module manufacturer specify the specific grounding methods that are to be used and either provide or specify the hardware to be used. These methods and the hardware will be evaluated during the listing of the module. It is likely that thread-cutting or thread-forming screws will no longer be used.

In the meantime, installers have to struggle with the existing hardware and instructions, even when they are poor. Suitable grounding hardware has been identified.

For those modules that have been supplied with inadequate or unusable hardware or no hardware at all, here is a way to meet the intent of the *Code* and UL Standard 1703.

For those situations requiring an equipment-grounding conductor larger than 10 AWG, a lay-in tin plated copper direct burial lug with a stainless-steel #10 screw, nut, flat washers, Belleville spring and lock washers can be used to attach a direct burial lay-in lug to the module frame at the point marked for grounding. See figure C-1. Before attaching the lug to the module, a stainless-steel brush should be used to remove any anodizing, oxidation, or clear coating from the aluminum module frame, and a thin coat of anti-oxidant film should be placed on the clean aluminum surface. The flat washers are required to prevent the lock washers from digging into the soft copper of the tin plated lug or the aluminum of the module frame. The Belleville washer provides uniform tension, and a torque screwdriver should be used for all electrical connections. See figure C-2. Some new grounding lugs have been listed for use without the anti-oxidant compound since the design of the lug penetrates the oxidation, but these should be evaluated with a specific module because of the varying thickness of the anodizing and clear coat on the modules. It is not acceptable to use the hex-head, green grounding screws (even when they a have 10-32 threads) because they are not suitable for outdoor exposure and will eventually corrode. The same can be said for other screws, lugs, and terminals that are not suitable for outdoor applications.

The direct burial lay-lugs are tin-plated lugs made of solid copper with a stainless-steel screw. They accept a 4 AWG to 14 AWG copper conductor. They are listed for direct burial use (DB) and outdoor use and can be attached to aluminum structures (the tin plate allows this). The much cheaper tin-plated aluminum lay-in lugs look identical, but

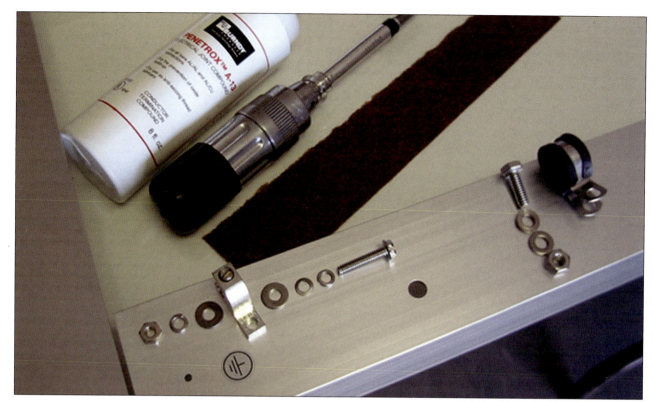

PHOTO 2 Connecting tin-plated copper lay-in lug to aluminum

have a plated screw, and are not listed for outdoor use. If the module grounding is to be done with a 14 AWG to 10 AWG conductor, then the lay-in lug may not be needed.

What size conductor should be used? The minimum *Code* requirement is for the equipment grounding conductor for PV source and output circuits to be sized to carry 1.25 times the short-circuit currents at that point. While this may allow a 14 AWG conductor between modules, a conductor this small would require physical protection between the grounding points. Some inspectors will allow a 10 AWG bare conductor to be routed behind the modules from grounding point to grounding point if the conductors are well protected from damage, as they would be in a roof-mounted array. If needed, an 8 AWG or 6 AWG sized conductor may be required (to meet the *Code* or to satisfy the inspector) and then the lay-in lugs or other listed grounding device should be used (690.45 and 690.46).

It is desirable to use the module mounting structure for grounding. Rack manufacturers have been urged to get their products listed as field-installable grounding devices, and some progress is being made in this area. UL Outline of Investigation 2703 deals with racks and module mounting systems. It evaluates the electrical and mechanical properties of the rack or mounting structure and verifies that the rack may be used as an equipment-grounding conductor for multiple modules. However, it does not necessarily evaluate the electrical connection between a specific module and the rack unless tested and evaluated with that module. Changes to UL Standard 1703 in 2012 require that the module manufacturer modify the instruction manuals to allow alternate grounding methods and specifically list these grounding methods and how they are to be applied in the module instruction manual.

The *Code* allows metal structures to be used for grounding and even allows the paint or other covering to be scraped away to ensure a good electrical contact. Numerous types of electrical equipment have parts that are grounded with sheet metal screws and star washers. This works (particularly in the factory environment) on common metals like steel, but not on aluminum due to the rapid oxidation.

Module manufacturers are being encouraged to make that aluminum connection in the factory and to provide a copper-compatible terminal in the j-box or on the frame as is done with the older 300-watt Schott modules.

Appendix C — Grounding PV Modules

Appendix D

Conductor Sizing and Overcurrent Device Ratings

Historically, most residential and light commercial electrical wiring and inspections of these systems have involved indoor wiring at room temperatures (30°C (86°F) or less). The ampacity tables in *NEC* Section 310.15 and Table 310.16 were developed with those conditions in mind. The commonly used molded case circuit breaker is rated for use with conductors with 75°C insulation and they have a rated maximum operating temperature of 40°C.

With these conditions and equipment characteristics in mind, the typical electrician has generally just used the 75°C insulated conductor ampacity tables in Table 310.16 and not bothered too much with temperature corrections (310.15) and terminal temperature limits [110.14(C)] since they were not necessary or were included in the tables being used.

However, direct current (dc) PV conductors normally operate in an environment that is too hot for conductors with 75°C insulation. Conductors with 90°C insulation must be used and appropriate temperature and conduit fill corrections must be applied along with verifying that connected equipment terminal temperatures (60° or 75°C) are not exceeded. To do otherwise and use the shortcuts of the old days will result in conductors that may be larger than *Code* requirements resulting in unnecessary costs.

Throughout the *Code*, circuits are sized based on 125% of the continuous load plus the noncontinuous load. See 210.19(A)(1) and 215.2(A)(1). This requirement establishes a situation where conductors and overcurrent devices are not subjected to more than 80% of rating. (Note: 1/1.25 = 0.80).

Electricians typically use the 125% factor and then apply the conditions of use factors (temperature and conduit fill) sequentially. The *NEC*, in a careful reading of 210.19(A)(1) and 215.2(A)(1), does not require that both factors be applied at the same time. See the 125% requirement below.

In the *Code*, we have at least two or three requirements that must be met in sizing conductors.

First is the definition of *ampacity* found in Article 100. Ampacity is "the current in amperes that a conductor can carry continuously under the conditions of use without exceeding its temperature ratings."

Next is the 125% requirement: "The minimum feeder circuit conductor size, before the application of any adjustment or correction factor, shall have an allowable ampacity not less than the noncontinuous loads plus 125 percent of the continuous loads."

Then: Section 110.14(C) requires that the temperature of the conductor in actual operation not exceed the temperature rating of terminals on the connected equipment.

An added requirement for any listed equipment such as overcurrent devices is that they not be used in a manner that deviates from the listing or labeling on the product [110.3(B)]. Most PV combiners operating outdoors in the sunlight will have internal temperatures that exceed the 40°C rated operating temperatures of commonly used fuses and circuit breakers.

The following method of determining ampacity meets the three *Code* requirements above and finds the smallest conductor that can be used to meet these requirements. It also determines the rating of the overcurrent device where required. It is consistent with the requirements found in Article 690 and elsewhere in the *Code*.

Step 1. Determine the maximum circuit current (690.8(A))

PV dc circuits and PV ac circuits are not "load" circuits so we will use the term *current* instead of *load*. For *Code* calculations, all dc and ac PV currents are considered continuous and are based on worst-case outputs or are based on safety factors applied to rated outputs. The term "maximum" currently is used in Article 690 instead of the term "continuous" current used elsewhere in the *Code*. The daily variation in these currents is ignored.

A. PV DC Circuits

In the dc PV source and dc PV output circuits, the maximum currents are defined as 1.25 times the rated short-circuit current I_{sc} (marked on the back of the module). If a module had an I_{sc} of 7.5 amps, the maximum current would be 7.5 x 1.25 = 9.375 amps [690.8(A)(1)].

If three strings of modules (module I_{sc} = 8.1 amps) were connected in parallel through a fused dc combiner, the PV output circuit of the combiner would have an I_{sc} of 3 x 8.1 = 24.3 amps (690.8(A)(2)) and the maximum current would be 24.3 x 1.25 = 30.375 amps [690.8(A)(2)].

B. AC Inverter Output Circuits

In the ac output circuits of a utility-interactive inverter or the ac output circuit of a stand-alone inverter, the continuous current is taken at the full power rated output of the inverter. It *is not* measured at the actual operating current (which may be a small fraction of the rated current due to a small PV array connected to a large inverter) of the inverter. Usually the rated current is at the nominal output voltage (120, 208, 240, 277, or 480 volts). The rated output current is usually specified in the manual, but may be calculated by dividing the rated power by the nominal voltage. For stand-alone inverters, which can provide some degree of surge current, it is the rated power that can be delivered continuously for three hours or more [690.8(A)(3)].

In some cases, the inverter specifications will give a rated current that is higher than the rated power divided by the nominal voltage. In that situation, the higher current should be used. This higher current has usually been determined at a lower-than-normal line voltage.

For a utility-interactive inverter operating at a nominal voltage of 240 volts and a rated power of 2500 watts, the continuous current would be:

2500W/240V=10.4A.

A stand-alone inverter with a model number of 3500XPLUS operates at 120 volts and can surge to 3500 watts for 60 minutes. However, it can only deliver 3000 watts continuously for three hours or more. The rated output current would be:

3000W/120V = 25A

C. Battery Currents

The currents between a battery and an inverter in either a stand-alone system or a battery-backed up utility-interactive system must be based on the rated output power of the inverter (continuous for three hours or more) at the lowest input battery voltage that can provide that output power [690.8(A)(4)].

This current is usually marked on the inverter or found in the specifications.

It can be calculated by taking the rated output power, dividing it by the lowest battery voltage that can sustain that power, and also by dividing by the inverter dc-to-ac conversion efficiency at that battery voltage and power level. For example: A 4000-watt inverter can operate at that power with a 44-volt battery input voltage and has a dc-to-ac conversion efficiency (inverting mode) of 85 percent. The dc continuous current will be:

4000W/44V/0.85 = 107A

On single-phase stand-alone inverters, the dc input current is rarely smooth and may have 120

Hz ripple current (RMS-root mean square) that is larger than the calculated continuous current. The inverter technical specifications should list the greatest continuous current.

Step 2. Calculate the rating of the overcurrent device, where required.

Since PV modules are current-limited, overcurrent devices are frequently not needed for one or two strings of PV modules connected in parallel. In systems with three or more strings of modules connected in parallel, overcurrent devices are usually required.

A. Rating Determined from Maximum Currents

The overcurrent device rating is determined by taking the maximum current for any of the circuits listed in Step 1 and increasing that maximum current by 125% (or by multiplying by 1.25). Non-standard values should be rounded up in most cases.

In a very few rare cases, an overcurrent device *installed in an enclosure* or an assembly may be tested, certified and listed *as an assembly* for operation at 100% of rating. The author knows of no overcurrent devices installed in an enclosure for PV systems that have such a rating.

B. Operating Temperature Affects Rating

Overcurrent devices are listed for a maximum operating temperature of 40°C (104°F). PV combiner boxes operating in outdoor environments may experience ambient temperatures as high as 50°C. Exposed to sunlight, the internal temperatures may reach or exceed 55–60°C. Any time, the operating temperature of the overcurrent device exceeds 40°C, it may be subject to nuisance trips at current values lower than its rating. In this situation, the manufacturer must be consulted to determine an appropriate derating. At high operating temperatures an overcurrent device with a higher rating will activate at the desired current.

Step 3. Select a conductor size.

The conductor selected for any circuit must meet both the ampacity rule and the 125% rule. The correctly sized cable is the larger of A or B below.

Example 1: Three (3) conductors are in a conduit in a boiler room where the temperature is 40°C.

The maximum current in all three conductors is 50 amps. A copper, 90°C insulated cable is specified.

A. Ampacity Requirement

The conductor after corrections for conditions of use must have an ampacity equal to or greater than the continuous current found in Step 1.

Temperature correction factor = 0.91
Conduit fill correction factor = 1.0

Required ampacity at 30°C is 50/0.91/1.0 = 54.9 amps and this would require an 8 AWG cable.

B. 125% Requirement

The cable must have an ampacity of 125% of the maximum current established in Step 1.

1.25 x 50 = 62.5 amps and this would indicate a 6 AWG cable.

The 6 AWG cable is the larger of the two and is required.

Example 2: Now there are six (6) conductors in the conduit and the temperature has increased to 50°C. The maximum current is still 50 amps.

Temperature correction factor = 0.82
Conduit fill factor = 0.8

Ampacity Rule: 50/0.8/0.82 = 76.2 amps and a 4 AWG cable is needed
125% Rule: 1.25 x 50 = 62.5 amps calling for a 6 AWG cable.

The 4 AWG cable is the larger of the two and must be used.

Step 4. Terminal temperature limits.

The terminal temperature limits marked on the equipment must be used. If no temperatures are marked, then a 60°C limit is used for circuits rated at 100 amps or less or cables 14-1 AWG. For circuits rated greater than 100 amps and for conductors greater than 1 AWG, a 75°C terminal temperature limit will be used. 110.14(C).

The following method is a terminal *temperature estimation* method and *is not* an ampacity calculation method. It is used after the conductor size has been selected based on the ampacity calculation.

Take the conductor size in Step 3 above. Find the lowest terminal temperature limit for this conductor at any termination. Use that terminal temperature limit (either 60°C or 75°C) to enter the ampacity Table 310.16 [310.15(B)(16) in the 2011 NEC]. For the conductor size selected, read out the current in the correct column, either the 60°C column or the 75°C column. There are no temperature adjustments or conduit fill adjustments in this estimation process.

The current from the table must be equal to or greater than 125% of the maximum current. And, if the conductor meets this requirement, then the terminal temperatures are going to be less than the 60°C or 75°C limit for that conductor and that maximum current. The 125% factor is a fudge factor that accounts for many items not calculated in this simplified temperature *estimation* process.

Example 3. Take the 6 AWG conductor and 50 amps of maximum current used in example 1 above. This conductor is connected to a terminal with a 60°C marking.

From Table 310.16/[310.15(B)(16)], a 6 AWG conductor in the 60°C column can carry a current of 55 amps.

1.25 x 50 = 62.5 amps. This is larger than the 55 amps from the table and this terminal will be heated above 60°C.

If we increase the conductor size to 4 AWG, the table gives us 70 amps, which is greater than 62.5 and the terminal will stay below 60°C.

Example 4. Use the 4 AWG conductor selected in example 2 connected to a terminal with a 75°C temperature limit. The maximum current is 50 amps.

1.25 x 50 = 62.5A.

A 4 AWG conductor in the 75°C column of Table 310.1 in as part of your identity I a(16)] shows a current of 85 amps. Since this is greater than the 62.5 amps, the conductor will operate cooler than the 75°C terminal temperature limit. No increase in conductor size is necessary.

Step 5. Verify that the overcurrent device protects the conductor selected under the conditions of use.

Where an overcurrent device is required, it must protect the conductor under operating conditions (conditions of use). Conductors may be protected using the round up allowance found in 240.4(B).

> ## Looking forward to 2014
>
> PV ampacity conductor requirements were well defined in the 2008 *NEC*. Now, in the 2014 *NEC*, other sections of the code have been modified to better clarify the ampacity requirements for branch circuits (210.19(A)(1)) and feeders (215.2(A)(1).
>
> **Battery systems.** The multimode inverter has now been defined in 690.2. This type of inverter is used in utility-interactive PV systems that have battery backup. It has one ac output that is purely utility-interactive and is connected to the utility circuits in the premises wiring system as any other utility-interactive inverter. Another output of the inverter is a stand-alone output and operates as a voltage source using energy from the connected batteries and/or the PV system. This stand-alone output does not go to zero when the load is disconnected as the utility interactive output does when it is disconnected from the utility voltage.
>
> **Overcurrent Devices.** A few overcurrent devices have been listed as PV fuses or PV circuit breakers and may have a rating valid at 50°C [See 690.9(D)] Where possible, these higher temperature overcurrent devices should be used in combiners (now defined as dc combiners in 690.2) that are exposed to solar heating in the outdoor environment. Of course, even the 50° C internal temperature may be exceeded in many installations.
>
> **DC-to-DC Converters.** The maximum current for these devices shall be the rated continuous output current rating. However, new devices of this type may be connected to the module and inverter in a manner that changes this number, so it is important to always follow the instruction manual for such products.

Appendix D — Conductor Sizing and Overcurrent Device Ratings

Example 5. A circuit has a maximum current of 70 amps. After conditions of use (4 conductors in the conduit, 48°C) are applied, a 3 AWG, 90°C conductor is selected to meet all ampacity and 75°C terminal temperature requirements.

The ampacity after conditions of use have been applied is:

$$115 \times 0.8 \times 0.82 = 75.4A$$

The required minimum overcurrent device for this level of maximum current is

$$70 \times 1.25 = 87.5A$$

A 90-amp overcurrent device would typically be used. A few people have suggested using an 80-amp overcurrent device, but that would result in running it at more than 80% of rating and in dc PV circuits could result in nuisance trips during short periods of cloud enhanced irradiance.

However, the largest overcurrent device that could be used to protect the 3 AWG conductor with an ampacity of 75.4 amps is an 80-amp overcurrent device and a 90-amp overcurrent device is the smallest allowed in this circuit.

The conductor size would have to be increased to 2 AWG for full compliance with *NEC* requirements.

The ampacity of a 2 AWG, 90°C conductor under the conditions of use is:

$$130 \times 0.8 \times 0.82 = 85.28A$$ and with the allowed round up, the next standard value of fuse is 90 amps.

The 2-AWG conductor can be protected by the required 90-amp overcurrent device.

Appendix E

690.64(B)/705.12(D)
LOAD-SIDE CONNECTIONS FOR UTILITY-INTERACTIVE PV INVERTER

This section of *Code* up to and including the *2011 NEC* was written to address a general condition where any panelboard busbar or conductor might be fed by multiple sources of power that are connected to the busbar or conductor through overcurrent devices. There are no restrictions in this *Code* requirement as to the particulars of any specific installation. There are no restrictions on where the multiple power sources might be connected on the busbar or conductor nor are there any limits on the number of overcurrent devices. There are no restrictions on the loads connected to the busbar or conductor either in terms of their connection point or the rating of the overcurrent device. When applying this requirement, no assumptions should be made as to the configuration of the circuit with respect the location of taps and the number, magnitude and locations of any sources or loads.

This is the manner in which many *Code* requirements are formulated. The requirement is written in general terms and then the general requirement is modified by exceptions (restrictions or allowances) or additions to the requirement.

In at least five code cycles, various changes and modifications have been proposed to change the basic requirement and wording. CMP-13 and now CMP-4 (2011 and subsequent editions of the *Code*) have ruled that the *only* way to protect this general busbar or conductor, that has no restrictions, is that the busbar or conductor must have an ampacity equal to or greater than the sum of the ratings of all overcurrent devices "supplying" that busbar or conductor.

As the time progresses, we have seen various wiring configurations for that general, unrestricted, busbar or conductor that might allow exceptions to the basic requirements. These wiring configurations are discussed among inspectors, electricians, conductor and panelboard manufacturers and, as they are vetted to be safe, proposals are made to change the *NEC*. These are in the form of exceptions or modifications to the basic requirements.

This process is not unique to 690.64(B)(2)/705.12(D)(2) and similar actions have been taken throughout the *NEC*.

With respect to 690.64(B)(2)/705.12(D)(2), it has long been recognized that if there are only two supply overcurrent devices and that they are at opposite ends of the busbar or conductor, then even if unrestricted loads or load taps are added between the two supply overcurrent devices, there is nowhere on the conductor or busbar where the currents may exceed the rating of the largest overcurrent device.

A change was accepted in the *2008 NEC* that recognizes this fact and requires that in a panelboard, if the two supply overcurrent devices are at opposite ends of the busbar, the sum of the ratings of the busbar may exceed the current rating of the busbar by 20%. The assumption is made that actual load on the panel will not exceed the panel rating in most residential and commercial locations. Unfortunately, actual experience dictates that plug loads are essentially unrestricted and unmonitored and may result in loads higher than calculated by the installing electrician.

A related proposal was made for the *2011 NEC* that would apply to end-fed conductors that have a restriction that they not be tapped for either loads or supplies. If this proposal were accepted, (it was rejected), then the conductor would need an ampacity only as high as the highest rating of one of the connected supply overcurrent devices.

The information in the following paragraph is technical in nature and may be subject to further investiga-

tion. It gives some indication that the Code may not be as conservative as many feel it is.

While this situation of connecting supply overcurrent devices at opposite ends may be safe for restricted conductors, it may not be suitable for busbars in panelboards, even though this allowance **is in the 2008 NEC***. Panelboards are subject to busbar current limitations and are also subject to thermal limitations due to the heating associated with the thermal trip elements in the common thermal/magnetic molded-case circuit breakers. For example a 100-amp, 120/240-V panelboard is tested during the listing process with a 100 amp main breaker and two 100-amp load breakers (one per phase) mounted directly below the main breaker. The ambient temperature is raised to 45 degrees Celsius, the input and output currents are set at 100 amps, the temperature is allowed to stabilize, and the panel must pass this test with no deformation of any parts. The internal thermal load is related to the heat produced by 400 amps passing through circuit breaker trip elements. If we add a backfed PV breaker pair, for example 50 amps, at the bottom of the panel, and if the loads on the panel were increased to 150 amps, no breakers would trip, no busbars would be overloaded, but the thermal load in the panel would be that associated with 600 amps, not the 400 amps the panel was designed and listed for. Panel manufacturers have stated that these panels may not be able to pass UL listing tests with those excessive thermal loads.*

How likely is it that increased loads would occur at the same time as high daytime PV outputs? No one knows, but the possibility exists and some inspectors report warm/hot load centers (without PV input) that may be operating already close to the rating of the main breaker.

Exceptions were proposed to 690.64(B)/705.12(D) to allow more flexible installations. These exceptions place restrictions or allowances on the general conditions of an unrestricted busbar or conductor. The restrictions keep the various installations safe.

For example, the 2008 NEC 690.64(B)(2) requirement says to add the ratings of all breakers supplying current to the panel. This would include the main plus all backfed PV breakers. Assume that it is desired to combine the outputs of two inverters in a dedicated PV ac combining panel with two 40-A breakers. An 80-A main breaker would be needed. The sum of all breakers would be 160 amps, necessitating a 200-A panel to meet 690.64(B)(2). However, if an exception (restriction) were added that prevented any loads from being added to the panel, then the maximum current that the busbar would ever see would be limited to the sum of the PV breakers. The panel could then be rated at 80 A or 100 A—still safe, and less costly.

In summary, 690.64(B)(2)/705.12(D)(2) is written as an unrestricted requirement for sizing conductors and busbars. The conductor or busbar is protected for any combination of loads and/or multiple sources and locations of loads or sources connected to the busbar or conductor.

Unfortunately, the proposals for revisions of 690.64(B)/705.12(D) in the 2011 *NEC* were not accepted.

An AHJ may certainly look at a specific installation consisting of a specific set of supply breakers, loads, and locations of the same and evaluate the ampacity requirements of the conductors or busbar. If an alternate methods and materials (AMM) approval is issued to allow a deviation from the wording of the *NEC*, then the AMM approval might also include instructions to the installer to modify the installation in a way to minimize the possibility of future changes to the installation that might violate the exceptions (restrictions). For example, a "No Loads Allowed" placard might be required on an ac PV inverter combining panel when an AMM approval has allowed the rating of the panel as either the main breaker rating or the sum of the PV breakers, whichever is greater. Another example (proposed for the *2011 NEC but not accepted*) is to allow a conductor fed from supply breakers at each end, to have an ampacity of the greater breaker rating, not the sum of the breakers, when the conductor is marked, "Multiple Power Sources—Do Not Tap" every ten feet where the conductor is accessible.

Looking forward to 2014

See Appendix H for a detailed description of the changes to 705.12(D) in the 2014 *NEC*.

Appendix F

FUSING OF DC PV MODULE CIRCUITS IN UTILITY-INTERACTIVE PV SYSTEMS

In most electrical systems, the *National Electrical Code (NEC)* requires every ungrounded circuit conductor to be protected from overcurrents that might damage that conductor. Overcurrent protective devices (OCPD), either fuses or circuit breakers, provide that function. However, some of the smaller utility-interactive PV systems may not need OCPD in the dc circuits that are connected to the PV modules.

The *NEC* assumes that each ungrounded conductor is connected to some source of overcurrents that might potentially damage that conductor under fault conditions. This source could be a power supply, a utility service, or a battery that supplies currents in excess of the ampacity rating of the conductor. The *NEC*, in 240.21, requires that the conductors be protected at their source of supply. PV modules are current-limited devices, and their worst-case, continuous outputs for *Code* calculations are 1.25 times the rated short-circuit current. Therefore the module cannot generate sufficient current to damage the conductor attached to it in a short-circuit condition. An exception to Section 690.9(A) allows conductors and PV modules to be used without OCPD where there are no sources of external currents that might damage that conductor or PV module.

Additionally, UL Standard 1703 requires that modules must have an *external* series OCPD if *external* sources of current can damage the *internal* module conductors. The module can be damaged if reverse currents are forced through the module (due to an external or internal fault) that are in excess of the values of the maximum series fuse marked on the label on the back of the module. Again, if there are no sources of external currents that exceed this marked value, then no OCPD is needed to protect the internal module wiring.

External sources of current (apart from the module or series-connected strings of modules) vary from system to system. These currents can originate from modules or series-connected strings of modules that are connected in parallel to the module of interest, from batteries in the system, or from utility currents backfeeding through utility-interactive inverters.

In systems with batteries and charge controllers, the batteries are a very predominate source of currents and, generally, OCPD will be required on each module or series-connected string of modules. Generally, only one OCPD will be required to protect all modules connected in a single series string. A properly sized and located OCPD will protect not only the conductors, but also the modules from external overcurrents [690.9(E)].

In utility-interactive systems, a few inverter designs may be capable of allowing current from the utility to flow backwards through the inverter

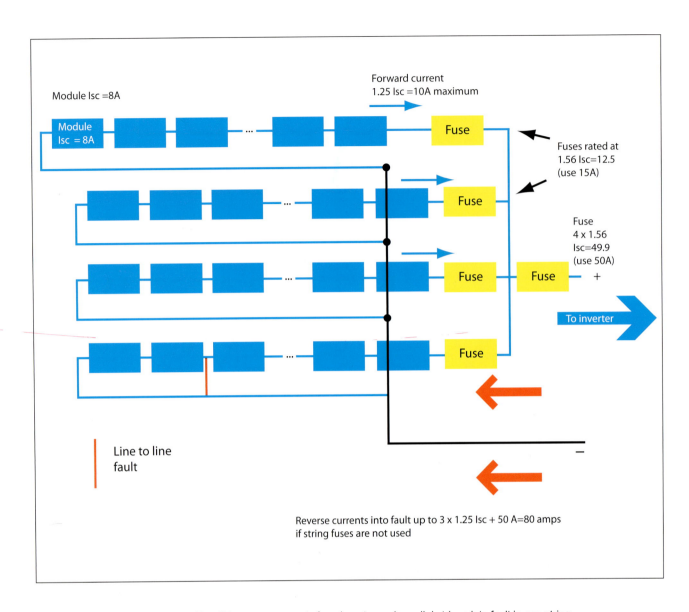

FIGURE F-1 Part of large system. Possible reverse currents from inverter and parallel strings into fault in one string.

into faults in the PV array. Systems using these types of inverters would typically require OCPD at the inverter dc inputs or OCPD on each string of modules or OCPD in both locations (see figure F-1). Many of the smaller utility-interactive inverters (below about 6 kW) are designed so that they cannot backfeed currents from the utility into array faults. However, there are currently no specific tests in the UL 1741 to validate the lack of backfeeding from the utility, so a manufacturer's certification should be obtained that the inverter cannot backfeed from the utility into an array dc wiring fault.

String fuses are required and an inverter fuse is required if inverter can backfeed into fault in dc system.

The general case — for most larger PV systems

The most common situation occurs in systems where there are multiple strings of modules connected in parallel. The non-faulted strings may be able to supply sufficient overcurrents (through the parallel connection) to damage either the conductors or the modules in the faulted strings. A basic question is: How many PV modules or strings of modules can be connected in parallel and still meet the *National Electrical Code (NEC)* and Underwriters Laboratories (UL) requirements (marked on the back of each module) before an OCPD is needed on each module/string of modules? UL marks the modules based on reverse-current tests. The *NEC* requires that the manufacturer's instructions and

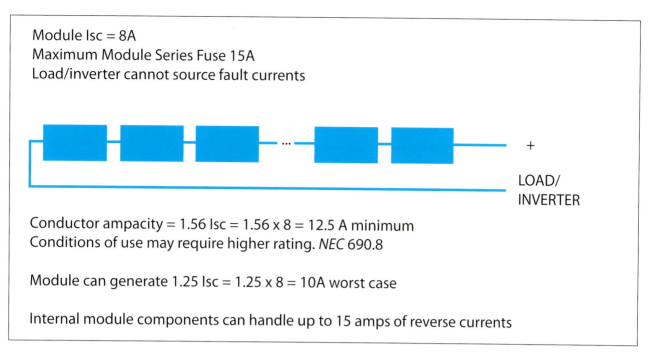

FIGURE F-2 Single string of PV modules. No external source of overcurrents that can damage the modules or the conductors. No overcurrent protection required. *NEC* 690.9(A) Exception

labels be followed [110.3(B)]. The intent of the module marking is to protect the conductors internal to the module at the marked level from reverse currents. This is a maximum value for the OCPD. Lesser values can be used as long as they meet the *NEC* requirement of 1.56*Isc to protect the conductor associated with the module or string of modules. In some cases, the value of the module protective overcurrent device is less than 1.56*Isc. This poses a *Code* conflict [110.3(B) vs. 690.8/9] and is an issue for UL or the listing agency to rectify.

Many installers of 12-, 24-, and 48-volt PV systems ignore the module OCPD requirement and connect modules/strings in parallel. Can it be done and how? David King, when he worked at Sandia National Laboratories, and the author have smoked a few modules and determined that the module OCPD requirement is valid — even at low voltages.

It is easy to see that in a one-string system, an OCPD is needed only when the inverter or battery is a source of overcurrents. No fusing would be required in a one-string system if there were no battery or inverter that could source overcurrents (see figure F-2).

Consider *n* modules or strings of modules connected in parallel. The *NEC* requires that an OCPD be installed in the combined paralleled output of all strings (modules) to protect the cable from reverse currents from batteries and back feed of ac currents through an inverter. In this case, we are assuming that the inverter or the batteries are a potential source of overcurrents. The OCPD will have a minimum rating of 1.56*n*Isc amps. It is sized at this value to allow maximum forward currents from the array to pass through without interruption and to keep the overcurrent device from operating at more than 80% of rating.

Examine a circuit where there are *n* modules/strings connected in parallel. Place a ground-fault in one module/string. Examine the sources of fault current that would affect that module string. Let us ignore current from the faulted module/string itself since the wiring in that string is already sized to carry all forward currents generated in the string.

First, there is the potential back feed current from the battery or the inverter in those systems with these components. It is limited to the *NEC* required OCPD of 1.56*n*Isc at its input. This current is added to the current from the remaining modules connected in parallel. In this case, the current is (n-1)*1.25*Isc. The 1.25 is required (representing the maximum current defined in [690.8]) because of daily-expected irradiance values that are greater than the STC-rated Isc.

Appendix F — Fusing of DC PV Module Circuits in Utility-Interactive PV Systems

I-fault = 1.56*n*Isc + (n-1) x 1.25*Isc

With a little algebra, the resulting fault current is:

I-fault = (2.81*n-1.25)*Isc amps. (Fault Current Equation)

Note that this equation does not account for rating roundup of the OCPD, so each system must be checked with the actual OCPD values.

If the module can pass the UL reverse current test at this I-fault value or greater and be so marked (the maximum protective series fuse on the label), then it is possible to parallel *n* modules/strings (pick your *n*) without a series OCPD for each module/string.

For example, a PV module is rated at 60 watts and has a maximum series OCPD requirement of 20-amps, which is marked on the back of the module. The Isc for this module is 3.8 amps. Here are the required calculations and checks for two strings in parallel.

The paralleled circuit OCPD installed at the output of the two paralleled strings will be 2*1.56*3.8 = 11.8 amps. Assume a 12-amp OCPD is used since the *NEC* now requires module/string OCPDs in one-amp increments up to 15 amps; fuses are available in these values except there is a jump from 10 to 12 and then to 15. This OCPD could potentially allow 12 amps of fault current to reach the faulted module/string from backfeed from a charge controller/battery or from the utility grid through a utility-interactive inverter. Another 1.25*3.8 = 4.75 amps could come from the parallel-connected module/string for a total of 16.75 amps. This is acceptable since this module is marked for 20 amps.

However, if we try to parallel three of these modules/strings, the fault current equation yields a fault current of 29+ amps that exceeds the 20-amp limit on the module. The single OCPD is 3*1.56*3.8 = 17.8 amps (since OCPDs at this rating are not common, a 20-amp OCPD must be used). The two parallel-connected modules contribute 2*1.25*3.8 = 9.5 amps for a total potential fault current of 29.5 amps. This is significantly above the maxim series protective fuse of 20 amps.

In most cases, it is not possible to parallel more than 2 modules/strings with a single OCPD unless the marked maximum series OCPD is very large in relation to Isc for the module. Some of the thin-film technologies may be able to do this and that will be an installation benefit for them.

Questions about driving voltages to produce these currents? The faults can occur anywhere in the module/string so a fault involving a single cell could be the trouble spot, and driving voltages over one volt could produce the reverse currents.

What about currents generated within the faulted module string? In the portion of the module/string below the fault (toward the grounded end of the module/string), the currents flow in the forward direction toward the fault and may or may not cause problems. As far as the contribution to the fault current is concerned, the contribution only appears in the fault path/arc and does not affect the ampacity of the cable. Above the fault (toward the ungrounded end), the currents in that portion of the module/string appear to oppose the external fault currents that are trying to reverse the flow of

Looking forward to 2014

Overcurrent Device Location. Section 690.9 has been revised to allow circuits with current-limited supplies such as module source circuits and utility-interactive inverter output circuits to be protected form overcurrents at the source of those external overcurrents. This allows the module and the module source circuit to have an overcurrent protective device (OCPD) located, not at the module, but at a dc combiner for multiple source circuits where currents from parallel connected source circuits can add to damaging currents. In a similar manner, the OCPD for a utility-interactive inverter ac output circuit is located at the end of the circuit connected to the potentially damaging, high current utility end of the circuit. See 690.9(D) for more.

Changes to UL 1703. UL Standard 1703 has been revised to require the marked OCPD on the back of the module to be no less than 1.56 times the marked Isc and that it be a standard, readily obtainable value of fuse or circuit breaker. The label no longer specifies "Maximum Fuse", but has been revised to show "Maximum Overcurrent Device, Where Required."

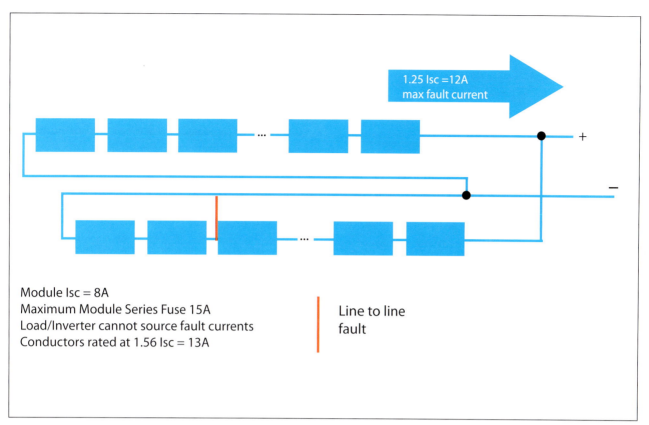

FIGURE F-3 Two strings in parallel. No source of overcurrents that can damage modules or conductors in faulted string. No backfeed from inverter. No overcurrent devices required. **NEC** 690.9(A) EX.

current, but the string is reversed biased, and the external driving currents are flowing. Since the location of the fault cannot be controlled ahead of time, worst-case currents must be assumed.

The increased marking value of 20 amps on the example module allows for two modules/strings to be connected in parallel and it does make it easier for the installer to use a single OCPD with larger cable to meet both the *NEC*-required cable protection and the UL-required module protection with one large OCPD instead of a two smaller OCPDs plus a larger OCPD.

Conductor ampacity must also be addressed if modules are going to be paralleled on a single OCPD. The conductors for each string must be able, under fault conditions, to carry the current from the other parallel strings (modules) plus the current that may be backfed from the inverter or battery. In the case with *n* strings in parallel and a single OCPD in the combined output, the conductor ampacities would be as follows:

Each of the string conductors would have to have an ampacity of 1.25 (n-1)*Isc + 1.56 n Isc. If the equation is factored, the required ampacity becomes A= (2.81*n-1.25)*Isc. As before, OCPD roundup is not considered and the values should be recalculated with actual OCPD values. The combined output-circuit conductors would require an ampacity of 1.56*n*Isc.

Modern, utility-interactive inverters

Many utility-interactive inverters on the market have redundant internal circuitry that prevents currents from being backfed through the inverter from the utility to faults in the PV array. This removes one source of currents in the above equation. With these products, it is possible to have two and sometimes more strings of modules in parallel with no OCPDs in the dc circuits. The inverter manufacturers should be contacted for information in this area. The above equations can be modified by deleting the combined-circuit OCPD and then solved to determine both the requirements for OCPDs and the necessary ampacity of the conductors.

In this case the current flowing through the forward fuse (n*1.56*Isc) is set equal to 0 (zero) or removed from the equation. In a system with *n* strings of modules connected in parallel, if one of the *n* strings develops a fault, the fault current is now reduced to:

I fault = (n-1) * 1.25 * Isc. For two strings in parallel, n = 2 and the fault current becomes

I fault = 1.25 Isc.

The *NEC* requires that all PV wiring generally be sized at 1.56 Isc. The required module series protective fuse is nearly always greater than 1.56 Isc.

Therefore, in a system with two strings of modules connected in parallel, there are no sources of fault current that exceed the ampacity of the conductors or the requirements for a module protective fuse. No dc string or array fuses would be needed. *NEC* Section 690.9(A) Exception applies [see figure F-3].

If there are more than two strings of modules connected in parallel, then the calculations outlined above will have to be made to ensure that (n-1)*1.25*Isc is less than the module series protective fuse value. If not, fuses should be used in each string. Again, the actual value of available fuses should be used in the calculations.

Appendix G

2005/2008/2011 NEC Photovoltaic Electrical Power Systems Inspector/Installer Checklist

The following checklist is an outline of the general requirements found in the *2005, 2008, 2011 National Electrical Codes* (*NEC*) — Article 690 for Photovoltaic (PV) Power Systems installations.

The checklist is only a guide and applies to any component used or installed in a PV system other than inside a listed, factory-assembled component.

The local authority having jurisdiction (AHJ) or inspector has the final say on what is or is not acceptable. Local codes may modify the requirements of the *NEC*.

This list should be used in conjunction with Article 690 and other applicable articles of the *NEC* and includes inspection requirements for both stand-alone PV systems (with and without batteries) and utility-interactive PV systems. Where Article 690 differs from other articles of the *NEC*, Article 690 takes precedence. [690.3]

References are generally to the *2005 and 2008 NEC* and other relevant documents. Changes related to *2011 NEC* are noted.

CHECKLIST FOR PHOTOVOLTAIC POWER SYSTEM INSTALLATIONS

1. PV ARRAYS
PV modules listed to UL Standard 1703? [110.3] (*2008 NEC*-690.4(D))

a. Mechanical Attachment
Modules attached to the mounting structure according to the manufacturer's instructions? [110.3(B)]
Roof penetrations secure and weather tight? [110.12]

b. Grounding
Each module grounded using the supplied hardware, the grounding point identified on the module and the manufacturer's instructions? Note: Bolting the module to a "grounded" structure usually will not meet *NEC* requirements [110.3(B)]. Array PV mounting racks are usually not identified as equipment-grounding conductors. (Note 690.43(C) and (D) in 2011 have additional provisions and allowances for grounding with mounting structures).

Properly sized equipment-grounding conductors routed with the circuit conductors? [690.45] Note differences between *2005, 2008 and 2011 NEC*.

c. Conductors
Conductor type? —If exposed: USE-2, UF (usually inadequate at 60°C), or SE, 90°C, wet-rated and sunlight-resistant. [690.31(B)] (*2008* and *2011 NEC* restrict exposed single-conductor wiring to USE-2 and listed PV/Photovoltaic Wire/Cable)—If in conduit: RHW-2, THWN-2, or XHHW-2 90°C, wet-rated conductors are required. [310.15]

Conductor insulation rated at 90°C [UL-1703] to allow for operation at 70°C+ near modules and in conduit exposed to sunlight (add 17-20°C to ambient temperature-*2005 NEC*), (See Table 310.15(B)(2) in the *2008 NEC* or Table 310.15(B)(3)(c) in the *2011 NEC*)

Temperature-derated ampacity calculations based on 156% of short-circuit current (Isc), and the derated ampacity greater than 156% Isc rating of overcurrent device? [690.8,9]

Note: Suggest temperature derating factors of 65°C in installations where the backs of the module receive cooling air (4" or more from surface) and 75°C where no cooling air can get to the backs of the modules. Ambient temperatures in excess of 40°C may require different derating factors.

(*2011 NEC* 690.8 substantially updates ampacity calculations to parallel calculations in other sections of the *NEC*.)

Portable power cords allowed only for tracker connections? [690.31(C), 400.3,7,8]

Strain reliefs/cable clamps or conduit used on all cables and cords? [300.4, 400.10]

Listed for the application and the environment? Fine stranded, flexible conductor cables properly terminated with terminals listed for such conductors? [690.31(E)(4)]

Cables and flexible conduits installed and properly marked? [690.31(E)]

Exposed conductors in readily accessible areas in a raceway if over 30 volts? (*2008 NEC* 690.31(A)) Note: Raceways cannot be installed on modules. Conductors should be installed so that they are not readily accessible.

2. OVERCURRENT PROTECTION

Overcurrent devices in the dc circuits listed for dc operation? If device not marked dc, verify dc listing with manufacturer. Auto, marine, and telecom devices are not acceptable.

Rated at 1.25 x 1.25 = 1.56 times short-circuit current from modules? [UL-1703, 690.8, module instructions] Note: Both 125% factors are now in the *NEC*, *but a duplicate 125% remains in the module instructions and should be removed in 2012 from the UL Standard.* Supplementary listed devices are allowed in PV source circuits only, but branch-circuit rated devices preferred. [690.9(C)].

Each module or series string of modules have an overcurrent device protecting the module? [UL-1703/*NEC* 110.3(B)] Note: Frequently, installers ignore this requirement marked on the back of modules. Listed combiner PV combiner boxes meeting this requirement are available. One or two strings of modules do not require overcurrent devices, but three strings or more in parallel will usually require an overcurrent device. The module maximum series fuse must be at least 1.56 I_{sc}.

Located in a position in the circuit to protect the module conductors from backfed currents from parallel module circuits or from the charge controller or battery? [690-9(A) FPN]

Smallest conductor used to wire modules protected? Sources of overcurrent are parallel-connected modules, batteries, and ac backfeed through inverters. [690-9(A)]

User-accessible fuses in "touch-safe" holders or fuses capable of being changed without touching live contacts? [690.16] Strengthened for 2011 to include distance between overcurrent device and disconnect.

3. ELECTRICAL CONNECTIONS

Pressure terminals tightened to the recommended torque specification?

Crimp-on terminals listed and installed with listed crimping tools by the same manufacturer? [110.3(B)]

Twist-on wire connectors listed for the environment (i.e. dry, damp, wet, or direct burial) and installed per the manufacturer's instructions?

Pressure lugs or other terminals listed for the environment? (i.e. inside, outside, wet, direct burial)

Power distribution blocks *listed* and not just UL Recognized?

Terminals containing more than one conductor listed for multiple conductors?

Connectors or terminals using flexible, fine-stranded conductors listed for use with such conductors? (*2008 NEC* 690.31(F), 690.74)

Locking (tool-required) on readily accessible PV conductors operating over 30 volts? (*2008 NEC* 690.33(C))

4. CHARGE CONTROLLERS

Charge controller listed to UL Standard 1741? [110.3] (*2008 NEC* 690.4(D)) Exposed energized terminals not readily accessible?

Does a diversion controller have an independent backup control method? [690.72(B)(1)]

5. DISCONNECTS

Disconnects listed for dc operation in dc circuits? Automotive, marine, and telecom devices are not acceptable.

PV Disconnect readily accessible and located at first point of penetration of PV conductors?

PV conductors outside structure until reaching first readily accessible disconnect unless in metallic raceway? [690.14, 690.31(F)]

Disconnects for all current-carrying conductors of PV source? [690.13]

Disconnects for equipment? [690.15/690.17]

Grounded conductors *not* fused or switched? Bolted disconnects OK [690.13].
Note: Listed PV Power Centers are available for 12, 24, and 48-volt systems and they contain charge controllers, disconnects, and overcurrent protection for entire dc system with possible exception of source circuit or module protective fuses.

6. INVERTERS (Stand-alone Systems)

Inverter listed to UL Standard 1741? [110.3] (*2008 NEC* 690.4(D)) Note: Inverters listed to telecommunications or other standards do not meet *NEC* requirements.

DC input currents calculated for cable and fuse requirements? Input current = rated ac output in watts divided by lowest battery voltage divided by inverter efficiency at that power level. [690.8(A)(4)] Note clarifications in the *2011 NEC*.

Cables to batteries sized 125% of calculated inverter input currents? [690.8(A)]

Overcurrent/Disconnects mounted near batteries and external to PV load centers if cables are longer than 4-5 feet to batteries or inverter?

High interrupt, listed, dc-rated fuses or circuit breakers used in battery circuits? AIR/AIC at least 20,000 amps? [690.71(C), 110.9]

No multiwire branch circuits where single 120-volt inverters connected to 120/240-volt load centers? [100–Branch Circuit, Multiwire], [690.10(C)]

7. BATTERIES

None are listed.

Building-wire type cables used? [Chapter 3] Note: Welding cables, marine, locomotive (DLO), and auto battery cables don't meet *NEC* requirements. Flexible, listed RHW, or THW cables are available. Article 400 flexible cables larger than 2/0 AWG are OK for battery cell connections, but not in conduit or through walls. [690.74, 400.8] Flexible, fine stranded cables require very limited, specially listed terminals. See stand-alone inverters for ampacity calculations.

Access limited? [690.71(B)]

Installed in well-vented areas (garages, basements, outbuildings, and not living areas)? Note: Manifolds, power venting, and single exterior vents to the outside are not required and should be avoided.

Cables to inverters, dc load centers, and/or charge controllers in conduit?

Conduit enters the battery enclosure below the tops of the batteries? [300.4]
Note: There are no listed battery boxes. Lockable heavy-duty plastic polyethylene tool boxes are usually acceptable

8. **INVERTERS** (Utility-interactive Systems)
Inverter listed to UL Standard 1741 and identified for use in interactive photovoltaic power systems? [*2008-NEC* 690.4(D), 690.60] Note: Inverters listed to telecommunications and other standards do not meet *NEC* requirements.

Backup charge controller to regulate the batteries when the grid fails? [690.72(B)(1)]

Connected to dedicated branch circuit with back-fed overcurrent protection? [690.64, *2008/2011 NEC* 705.12]

Listed dc and ac disconnects and overcurrent protection? [690.15,17]

Total rating of overcurrent devices *supplying* power to ac load center (main breaker plus backfed PV breaker) must be less than load-center rating (120% of rating in residences) [690.64(B)(2)]. The *2008 NEC* allows the 120% breaker total on commercial installations and residential system ONLY if the PV breaker is at the opposite end of the busbar from the main utility breaker. No change for 2011.

9. **GROUNDING**
Only one bonding conductor (grounded conductor to ground) for dc circuits and one bonding conductor for ac circuits (neutral to ground) for system grounding? [250] Note: The main dc bonding jumper will generally be located inside inverters as part of the ground-fault protection devices. On stand-alone systems, the dc bonding jumper may be in a separate ground fault detection and interruption device or may be built in to the charge controller.

AC and dc grounding electrode conductors connected properly? They may be connected to the same grounding electrode system (ground rod). Separate electrodes, if used, must be bonded together. [690.41,47] The *2008 NEC* in 690.47 allows a combined dc grounding electrode conductor and an ac equipment-grounding electrode, but the conditions and requirements are numerous. The *2011 NEC* clarifies and combines *2005 and 2008 NEC* 690.47(C) requirements.)

The *2008 NEC* 690.47(D) array-grounding requirement was removed in *2011 NEC*. Equipment grounding conductors properly sized (even on ungrounded, low-voltage systems)? [690.43, 45, 46]

Disconnects and overcurrent in both of the ungrounded conductors in each circuit on 12-volt, ungrounded systems or on ungrounded systems at any voltage? [240.20(A)], [690.41]

Bonding/grounding fittings/bushings used with metal conduits when dc system voltage is more than 250V dc? [250.97]. Grounding bonding bushings used where grounding electrode conductors are in metallic raceways?

10. **CONDUCTORS** (General)

    Standard building-wire cables and wiring methods used? [300.1(A)]

    Wet-rated conductors used in conduits in exposed locations? [100 Definition of Location, Wet]

    Conductor insulations other than black in color will not be as durable as black in the outdoor UV-rich environment.

DC color codes correct? They are the same as ac color codes—grounded conductors are white and equipment-grounding conductors are green, green/yellow, or bare. [200.6(A)] Ungrounded PV array conductors on ungrounded PV arrays will *not* be white in color.

11. **Markings.** All field-applied markings correct?

    690.5, 690.17, 690.10, 690.35, 690.51, 690.53, 690.54, 690.55, 690.56, 705.10, 705.12

For *NEC*- 2014 Checklist, see Appendix I

Appendix H

Load-Side PV Connections 705.12(D) in the 2014 NEC

Introduction

Through the exceptional efforts of the members of NFPA *NEC* Code Making Panel 4 working with the proposals and comments that were submitted for the 2014 *Code*, significant changes have been made to Section 705.12 (D), Load Side Connections for Utility-interactive PV Inverters. These changes will allow better understanding of the requirements for load side connections of utility interactive inverters and will clarify requirements that were not fully described in previous editions of the code. Not only will AHJs and plan reviewers benefit from these changes, the PV installer will also have significantly improved guidance in this area.

All material in quotations below is taken from the 2014 *National Electrical Code (NEC), ANSI/NFPA 70*. **Bold italics text** represent changes from the 2011 *NEC*.

Introductory Paragraph 705.12(D)

"**705.12(D) Utility-Interactive Inverters.** The output of a utility interactive inverter shall be permitted to be connected to the load side of the service disconnecting means of the other source(s) at any distribution equipment on the premises. Where distribution equipment, including ***switchgear***, switchboards, ***or*** panelboards, is fed simultaneously by a primary source(s) of electricity and one or more utility-interactive inverters, and where this distribution equipment is capable of supplying multiple branch circuits or feeders, or both, the interconnecting provisions for the utility-interactive inverter(s) shall comply with 705.12(D)(1) through (D)(**6**)."

The word switchgear has been added to the list of distribution equipment. And as in past editions of the *Code*, distribution equipment is not specifically defined. Of course, we all know what it means and numerous examples are usually given. But, we must also consider that distribution equipment in the form of junction boxes for taps or new panelboards can be added to the premises wiring at almost any location that is allowed by the code. So essentially connections for utility-interactive inverters can be made at many points on the load side circuits that are not in existing distribution equipment.

705.12 (D)(2) Bus or Conductor *Ampere* Rating

"*One hundred twenty-five percent of the inverter output circuit current shall be used in ampacity calculations for the following:*"

Note that the title of the section remains bus or conductor ratings and will apply to both as they are defined in the introductory paragraph. The first noteworthy change in this section is the use of a factor of 125% of the inverter rated output current in calculations for busbar ratings and conductor ampacity. In the previous code, the rating of the overcurrent device protecting the inverter output circuit was used in the calculations. This new allowance may slightly reduce the required busbar and conductor ratings required by the following calculations.

Feeders
Feeder Ampacity

"(1) Feeders. Where the inverter output connection is made to a feeder at a location other than the opposite end of the feeder from the primary source overcurrent device, that portion of the feeder on the load side of the inverter output connection shall be protected by one of the following:

(a) The feeder ampacity shall be not less than the sum of the primary source overcurrent device and 125 percent of the inverter output circuit current.

(b) An overcurrent device on the load side of the inverter connection shall be rated not greater than the ampacity of the feeder."

This section represents a significant change from past code requirements. It presents requirements for feeder size and overcurrent protection when the utility interactive inverter connection *is not* at the opposite end of the feeder from the utility connection.

PV Opposite Utility On the Feeder (Not addressed by *Code*)

Since, the situation where the PV connection *is* at the opposite end of the feeder is not addressed in the new requirements, we can assume (sometimes not a good thing to do) that there is no ampacity correction required on the feeder under that situation. The size of the existing feeder was determined by the existing overcurrent device protecting that circuit from utility currents. Consider the feeder carrying PV currents with fused disconnects in the feeder at various points.

Additionally, while locating the PV inverter output connection at the opposite end of the feeder from the utility source will prevent the feeder form being overloaded by additive currents, it is obvious that 125% of the rated inverter output current must not exceed either the rating of the utility-end overcurrent device or the ampacity of the existing feeder.

Existing Load Taps of the Feeder (Not addressed by *Code*)

However, if that existing feeder has been tapped for load(s), common sense would dictate a close look at the tap rules because now there are two sources of current that can feed the tap conductor and the tap rules and tap conductor size used initially may no longer be appropriate.

In (a), a PV connection is made to the feeder somewhere along the feeder, but not at the end opposite the utility connection. The portion of the feeder, from the connection point to the load end of the feeder can be subjected to currents that are additive and can be as high as the rating of the existing utility end overcurrent device protecting the feeder plus the output of the PV inverter. Hence, the conductor from the connection point to the load end of the feeder must have an increased ampacity equal to the sum of the existing overcurrent device protecting the feeder and 125% of the inverter output rating as noted in this section. See diagram H-1.

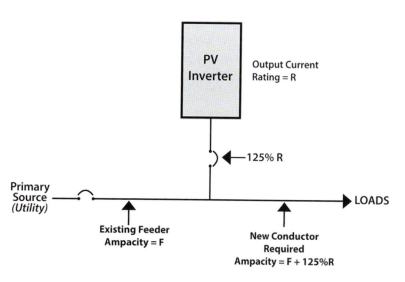

Diagram H-1. 705.12(D)(2)(1)(a) Increased feeder ampacity required.

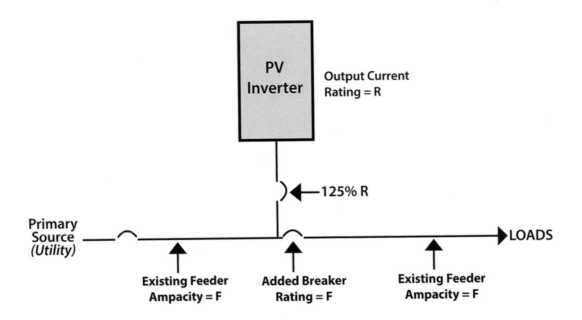

Diagram H-2. 705.12(D)(2)(1)(b) Additional breaker required.

In (b), an allowance is made to protect the existing feeder by installing an overcurrent device on the feeder on the load side of the connection point at the connection point. This allowance, with the added overcurrent protection rated the same as the existing feeder, will allow the existing feeder to be retained and not be replaced as may be required in (a). The addition of this overcurrent device will prevent excess load currents or faults from exceeding the ampacity of the feeder. See diagram H-2.

Inverter Output Circuit (the tap conductor) Size

> *"(2) Taps. In systems where inverter output connections are made at feeders, any taps shall be sized based on the sum of 125 percent of the inverter(s) output circuit current and the rating of the overcurrent device protecting the feeder conductors as calculated in 240.21(B)."*

Significant engineering analysis by code making panel members and others went into this change concerning the use of the tap rules in section 240.21 (B). While an overcurrent device and a disconnect are still required at the output of each utility-interactive inverter, that overcurrent protective device does not have to be at the tap point on the feeder. The tap rules allow the overcurrent device to be on the tap conductor at various distances from the connection point to the feeder. The inverter output overcurrent protective device is still required to be 125% of the inverter output rating, and of course, there may be rating round up involved in selecting an appropriate overcurrent device. However, when calculating the required ampacity of the tap conductor under the various tap rules, the actual factor of 125% of the inverter rated output current is used and not the overcurrent device rating. Again, this may yield slightly reduced conductor sizes. See diagram H-3.

Busbars

> *"(3) Busbars. One of the methods that follows shall be used to determine the ratings of busbars in panelboards.*

Busbar Rule (a)

> *(a) The sum of 125 percent of the inverter(s) output circuit current and the rating of the overcurrent device protecting the busbar shall not exceed the ampacity of the busbar.*

> *Informational Note: This general rule assumes*

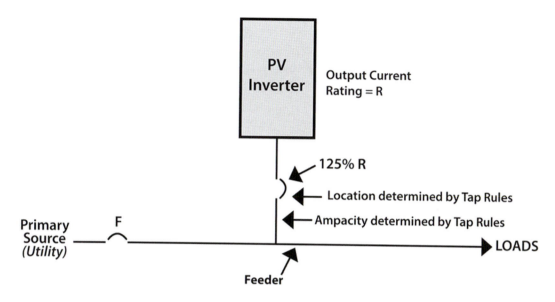

Diagram H-3. 705.12(D)(2)(2) Tap rules used to locate PV breaker and determine conductor ampacity.

This worst-case requirement presented in (a) assumes that the utility current through the existing main breaker and the current from the output of the utility-interactive inverter may add and that current may create an overload on the busbar. There are no restrictions on the location of the main utility breaker or the PV backfed breaker. If the busbar has a rating equal to the sum of these two values, then no overload would be possible.

It should be noted that reductions in the size of the utility breaker are not prohibited in this section and could be accomplished if allowed by other sections of the Code, load calculations and equipment limitations.

Busbar Rule (b)

"(b) Where two sources, one a utility and the other an inverter, are located at opposite ends of a busbar that contains loads, the sum of 125 percent of the inverter(s) output circuit current and the rating of the overcurrent device protecting the busbar shall not exceed 120 percent of the ampacity of the busbar. The busbar shall be sized for the loads connected in accordance with

no limitation in the number of the loads or sources applied to busbars or their locations."

Article 220. A permanent warning label shall be applied to the distribution equipment adjacent to the back-fed breaker from the inverter that displays the following or equivalent wording:

> **WARNING:**
> **INVERTER OUTPUT CONNECTION;**
> **DO NOT RELOCATE THIS**
> **OVERCURRENT DEVICE.**

The warning sign(s) or label (s) shall comply with 110.21(B)."

Section (b) is similar to the requirement found in previous editions of the code. If the two sources (utility and PV) are at opposite ends of the busbar, then the sum of those two sources can be as high as 120% of the busbar rating. With this location of sources, it is not possible to overload the busbar. Note that the busbar must be sized for the loads that are connected. The reason for the value of 120% is lost in history, but may be related to potential thermal overloading of the panelboard. The warning label is self-explanatory and the new requirement referring to section 110.21 (B) gives additional information on the specifics of the appearance and durability of the warning label.

Busbar Rule (c)

"(c) The sum of the ampere ratings of all overcurrent devices on panelboards, both load and supply devices, excluding the rating of the overcurrent device protecting the busbar, shall not exceed the ampacity of the busbar. The rating of the overcurrent device protecting the busbar shall not exceed the rating of the busbar. Permanent warning labels shall be applied to distribution equipment that displays the following or equivalent wording:

> **WARNING:**
> **THIS EQUIPMENT FED BY MULTIPLE SOURCES. TOTAL RATING OF ALL OVERCURRENT DEVICES, EXCLUDING MAIN SUPPLY OVERCURRENT DEVICE, SHALL NOT EXCEED AMPACITY OF BUSBAR.**

The warning sign(s) or label (s) shall comply with 110.21(B)."

Section (c) provides an alternate method of sizing the PV backfed breaker, or determining the size of the required busbar if the PV backfed breaker rating is known. This section will most likely be used when connecting PV to a subpanel or when sizing inverter ac combining panelboards. After excluding the main breaker from the utility, the sum of all remaining breakers, both load breakers and the PV supply breaker may not exceed the rating of the busbar. There are several aspects to this requirement that need close inspection and consideration.

First, the main breaker before the addition of any PV has been sized to protect the busbar from possible overload from utility currents. The main breaker will always be equal to or smaller than the busbar rating. For example, many load centers have a 125-amp busbar, but only a 100-amp main breaker. In a normal panelboard or load center, the ratings of the load breakers will total more than the rating of the main breaker or the busbar in nearly all circumstances. If this situation exists, then no PV can be added because the requirement cannot be met because the sum of the load breakers already exceeds the rating of the busbar. However, if the sum of the load breakers were equal to the rating of the busbar, that busbar would still be protected both by the main breaker and by the fact that excess current over the busbar could not be drawn through the load breakers. And again, under this condition, no PV backfed breaker could be added. However as the sum of the load breakers is reduced, there becomes an allowance for adding a backfed PV breaker with increasing ratings. In the extreme case, there could be a situation where there are no load breakers and only a single backfed PV breaker rated the same as the busbar. In any of these cases, no matter where the PV breaker is installed on the busbar, the supply and/or load currents cannot exceed the rating of the busbar.

But, it should be noted that in existing load centers, with the sum of the load breakers totaling more than the busbar rating, it is unlikely that load and load breakers can or will be removed.

And, of course, it would not be wise to install a backfed PV breaker that was larger than the main breaker in those instances where the busbar rating is larger than the main breaker. If this were done, the main breaker could trip from over currents through the larger PV breaker.

But, this section needs to be used with extreme caution because there is no restriction on the position of the backfed PV breaker. Suppose a 50 amp PV breaker were installed near the top of the 100 amp busbar in the load center near a 100 amp main breaker and there were 50 amps of load breakers. The code requirement is met with this configuration. However, what happens if someone disregards the warning label or the label simply falls off over time? I suspect that many jurisdictions are going to have to emphasize the permanent nature of that warning label to cover the materials that it is made of and the manner in which it is fixed to the panel board. Also, some consideration might be made to permanently covering unused panelboard breaker positions. It might be wise to adopt a local jurisdiction requirement that the backfed PV breaker always be installed as far as possible from the main utility breaker and an additional warning label as required in (b) be placed adjacent to this PV breaker, or other PV overcurrent device.

Photo H-1. Installation of voltage taps for measuring the electrical output of the PV systems. *Photo credit: Ruby Nahan, NREL*

Appendix H — Load Side PV Connections

Center-fed Panelboards and Multiple-ampacity busbars

"(d) Connections shall be permitted on multiple-ampacity busbars or center-fed panelboards where designed under engineering supervision that includes fault studies and busbar load calculations."

There was no provision in earlier codes to address center-fed panelboards or multiple-ampacity busbars and it was not possible to install the PV breaker at the opposite end of the busbar from the main breaker because there were two or more busbars connected to the main breaker. Section (d) was specifically added to the *2014 Code* to address the common situation where PV needs to be connected to a center-fed panelboard. Although not clearly stated, there was no intent to allow center-fed panelboards to be installed under sections (a) through (c) of 705.12(D)(3). PV connections are now allowed on center-fed panelboards and multiple-ampacity busbars under the conditions noted in this section. Engineering supervision typically indicates that the analysis of the PV connection will be made and stamped by a Professional Engineer. The load calculations will look not only at the breakers installed on the busbars, but also the loads connected to those breakers, and the possibility of installing additional breakers and loads in unused spaces in the panelboard. Fault studies may involve looking at the electrical time versus current profiles for each of the circuit breakers involved to ensure that all portions of the busbars will be protected under various fault scenarios from currents sourced both from the utility through the main breaker and from the PV system through the backfed PV breaker.

Marking (3), Suitable for Backfeed (4), and Fastening (5)

These sections are unchanged from the *2011 NEC*.

Wire Harness and Exposed Cable Arc-Fault Protection

"(6) A utility-interactive inverter(s) that has a wire harness or cable output circuit rated 240 V, 30 amperes, or less, that is not installed within an enclosed raceway, shall be provided with listed ac AFCI protection."

This requirement will apply mainly to micro-inverter systems that have inverter ac output cables and trunk cables that are not installed in conduit.

Summary

It is obvious that the new 705.12(D) requirements are significantly different from those in past years. While many of them make sense from an engineering point of view, the real world faced by inspectors and plan reviewers may be somewhat different where people typically ignore instructions, ignore the code, and ignore warning labels. On the other hand, PV systems have not changed significantly from 2011 to 2014 and the electrical systems they are being connected to have not changed significantly, so these new requirements might also be applied in jurisdictions using earlier editions of the Code by accepting alternate methods and materials waivers based on the 2014 *NEC* clarifications.

Appendix I

2014 NEC Photoviltaic Electrical Power Systems Inspector/Installer Checklist

The following checklist is an outline of the general requirements found in the *2014 National Electrical Code* (*NEC*) in Articles 690 and 705 that deal with Photovoltaic (PV) Power Systems installations.

The checklist is only a guide and applies to any component used or installed in a PV system other than devices inside a listed, factory-assembled component.

The local authority having jurisdiction (AHJ) or inspector has the final say on what is or is not acceptable. Local codes may modify the requirements of the *NEC*.

This list should be used in conjunction with Article 690, Article 705 and other applicable articles of the *NEC* and includes inspection requirements for both stand-alone PV systems (with and without batteries) and utility-interactive PV systems. Where Article 690 differs from other articles of the *NEC*, Article 690 or 705 takes precedence. (690.3)

CHECKLIST FOR PHOTOVOLTAIC POWER SYSTEM INSTALLATIONS

1. PV ARRAYS

PV modules listed to UL Standard 1703? [110.3, 690.4(B)]

a. Mechanical Attachment

Modules attached to the mounting structure according to the manufacturer's instructions? [110.3(B)]

Roof penetrations secure and weather tight? (110.12, 110.13)

b. Grounding

Each module grounded using the supplied hardware, the grounding point identified on the module and the manufacturer's instructions? Note: Bolting the module to a "grounded" structure usually will not meet *NEC* requirements [110.3(B)] and may not comply with the instructions for grounding the PV module. Array PV mounting racks are usually not identified as equipment-grounding conductors, unless certified/listed to UL Standard 2703. (690.43)

Properly sized equipment-grounding conductors routed with the circuit conductors? (690.45)

c. Conductors

Conductor type? —If exposed: USE-2 or PV wire for grounded PV arrays and PV wire for ungrounded PV arrays. Nearly all PV modules will have attached PV wire to allow the use in ungrounded PV arrays (690.35).

Conductor insulation rated at 90°C (UL-1703) to allow for operation at 70°C+ near modules and in conduit or cables exposed to sunlight [Table 310.15(B)(3)(c)]

Temperature-corrected ampacity calculations based on 125% of short-circuit current (Isc), and the corrected ampacity greater than 156% Isc rating of overcurrent device? (690.8, 9)
 Note: *Suggest* temperature derating factors of 65°C for conductors behind modules in installations where the backs of the module receive cooling air (4" or more from roof) and 75°C where no cooling air can get to the backs of the modules. Ambient temperatures in excess of 40°C may require different derating factors.

Portable power cords allowed only for tracker connections? (690.31(C), 400.3, 7, 8)

Strain reliefs/cable clamps or conduit used on all cables and cords? (300.4, 400.10)

Listed for the application and the environment? Fine stranded, flexible conductor cables properly terminated with terminals listed for such conductors? (110.14)

Cables and flexible conduits installed and properly marked? (690.31)

Exposed conductors in readily accessible areas in a raceway or guarded if over 30 volts? [690.31(A)] Note: Raceways cannot be installed on modules. Conductors should be installed so that they are not readily accessible (i.e., guarded).

2. OVERCURRENT PROTECTION

Overcurrent devices in the dc circuits listed for dc operation? If device not marked dc, verify dc listing with manufacturer. Auto, marine, and telecom devices are not acceptable.

Rated at 1.25 x 1.25 = 1.56 times short-circuit current from modules? (UL-1703, 690.8, module instructions). Overcurrent devices listed for PV applications are required. [690.9(D)].

Each module or series string of modules has an overcurrent device protecting the module? [UL-1703/*NEC* 110.3(B)] Note: Frequently, installers ignore this requirement marked on the back of modules. Listed combiner PV combiner boxes meeting this requirement are available. One or two strings of modules do not require overcurrent devices, but three strings or more in parallel will usually require an overcurrent device. The module maximum series fuse must be at least 1.56 I_{sc}. [690.9(A)]

Located in a position in the circuit to protect the module conductors from backfed currents from parallel module circuits or from the charge controller or battery? [690.9(A)]

Smallest conductor used to wire modules protected? Sources of overcurrent are parallel-connected modules, batteries, and ac backfeed through inverters. [690.9(A)]

User-accessible fuses in "touch-safe" holders or fuses capable of being changed without touching live contacts? Disconnects from all sources of voltage in dc combiners at the inverter? (690.16)

3. ELECTRICAL CONNECTIONS

Pressure terminals tightened to the recommended torque specification? [110.3(B)], (IN 110.14)

Crimp-on terminals listed and installed with listed crimping tools by the same manufacturer? [110.3(B)]

Twist-on wire connectors listed for the environment (i.e., dry, damp, wet, or direct burial) and installed per the manufacturer's instructions?

Pressure lugs or other terminals listed for the environment? (i.e., inside, outside, wet, direct burial)

Power distribution blocks *listed* and not just UL Recognized?

Terminals containing more than one conductor listed for multiple conductors?

Connectors or terminals using flexible, fine-stranded conductors listed for use with such conductors? (690.31(H), 690.74(A), 110.14)

Locking (tool-required) on readily accessible PV conductors operating over 30 volts? [690.33(C)]

4. CHARGE CONTROLLERS

Charge controller listed to UL Standard 1741? [690.4(B)]

Exposed energized terminals not readily accessible?

Does a diversion controller have an independent backup control method? [690.72(B)(1)]

5. DISCONNECTS

Rapid shutdown system installed? (690.12) Applied to inverter inputs, module outputs, batteries (where used), and combiner outputs?

Disconnects listed for dc operation in dc circuits? Automotive, marine, and telecom devices are not acceptable.

PV Disconnect readily accessible and located at first point of penetration of PV conductors?

PV conductors outside structure until reaching first readily accessible disconnect unless in metallic raceway? [690.13(A), 690.31(F)]

Disconnects for all current-carrying conductors of PV source? (690.13)

Disconnects for equipment? (690.15/690.17)

DC combiner have load break rated output disconnect internal or within 1.8 m (6 ft)? [690.15(C)]

Grounded conductors *not* fused or switched? Bolted disconnects OK (690.17(D)-EX 1 and 2)
   Note: Listed PV Power Centers are available for 12, 24, and 48-volt systems and they contain charge controllers, disconnects, and overcurrent protection for entire dc system with possible exception of source circuit or module protective fuses.

6. INVERTERS (Stand-alone Systems)

Inverter listed to UL Standard 1741? [110.3) 690.4(B)] Note: Inverters listed to telecommunications or other standards do not meet *NEC* requirements.

DC input currents calculated for cable and fuse requirements? Input current = rated ac output in watts divided by lowest battery voltage divided by inverter efficiency at that power level. [690.8(A)(4)]

Cables to batteries sized 125% of calculated inverter input currents? [690.8(A)]

Overcurrent/Disconnects mounted near batteries and external to PV load centers if cables are longer than 4–5 feet to batteries or inverter?

High interrupt, listed, dc-rated fuses or circuit breakers used in battery circuits? AIR/AIC at least 20,000 amps? [690.71(C), 110.9, 110.10]

No multiwire branch circuits where single

120-volt inverters connected to 120/240-volt load centers? (100–Branch Circuit, Multiwire), (690.10(C))

7. BATTERIES

None are listed.

Building-wire type cables used? (Chapter 3) Note: Welding cables, marine, locomotive (DLO), appliance wire material (AWM) and auto battery cables don't meet *NEC* requirements. Flexible, listed RHW, or THW cables are available. Article 400 flexible cables larger than 2/0 AWG are OK for battery cell connections, but not in conduit or through walls. (690.74, 400.8) Flexible, fine-stranded cables require limited-availability, specially listed terminals (110.14, 690.74). See stand-alone inverters for ampacity calculations.

Access limited? [690.71(B)]

Installed in well-vented areas (garages, basements, outbuildings, and not living areas)? Note: Manifolds, power venting, and single exterior vents to the outside are not required and should be avoided.

Have the conductor routing and protection requirements of 690.71(H) been met?

Cables to inverters, dc load centers, and/or charge controllers in conduit?

Conduit enters the battery enclosure below the tops of the batteries? (300.4) Note: There are no listed battery boxes. Lockable heavy-duty plastic polyethylene tool boxes are usually acceptable.

8. INVERTERS (Utility-interactive Systems)

Inverter listed to UL Standard 1741 and identified for use in interactive photovoltaic power systems? [690.4(B), 705.4] Note: Inverters listed to telecommunications and other standards do not meet *NEC* requirements.

Backup charge controller to regulate the batteries in systems with multimode inverters when the grid fails? [690.72(B)(1)]

Connected to dedicated branch circuit with back-fed overcurrent protection? [705.12(D)]

Listed dc and ac disconnects and overcurrent protection? (690.15, 17)

All requirements of 705.12(D) met?

9. GROUNDING

Only one bonding conductor (grounded conductor to ground) for dc circuits and one bonding conductor for ac circuits (neutral to ground) for system grounding? (250) Note: The main dc bonding jumper will generally be located inside inverters as part of the ground-fault protection devices. On stand-alone systems, the dc bonding jumper may be in a separate (690.5) ground-fault detection and interruption device or may be built in to the charge controller.

System/inverter grounding meets requirements of 690.47(C)?

Array grounded per 690.47(D)?

Equipment grounding conductors properly sized (even on ungrounded, low-voltage systems)? (690.43, 45, 46)

Disconnects and overcurrent in both of the ungrounded conductors in each circuit on 12-volt, ungrounded systems or on ungrounded systems at any voltage? (690.31)

Bonding-grounding fittings or bushings used with metal conduits when dc system voltage is more than 250V dc? (250.97). Grounding bonding bushings used where grounding electrode conductors are in metallic raceways and /or enclosures?

10. **CONDUCTORS** (General)

    Standard building-wire cables and wiring methods used? [300.1(A)]

    Wet-rated conductors used in conduits in exposed locations? (100, Definition of Location, Wet)

    Conductor insulations other than black in color will not be as durable as black in the outdoor UV-rich environment.

    DC color codes correct? They are the same as ac color codes: grounded conductors are white and equipment-grounding conductors are green, green/yellow, or bare. [200.6(A)] Ungrounded PV array conductors on ungrounded PV arrays will *not* be white in color.

11. **Markings.**

    All field-applied markings correct? [690.5, 690.7, 690.10, 690.13(B), 690.17(E), 690.31(B) & (G), 690.32(E), 690.35(F), 690.51, 690.53, 690.54, 690.55, 690.56, 690.71(H), 705.10, 705.12]

    Meet color and letter size requirements? (690.56)

Appendix J

A Brief Overview PV and the 2014 National Electrical Code

The *2014 National Electrical Code* has numerous changes in Article 690 and 705 that apply to photovoltaic (PV) power systems. Here is a brief overview some of those changes.

Article 690

690.2 Definitions. DC to DC Converters are defined, but little information will be found on how they are to be installed. The AHJs and the installer will have to rely on the instruction manual for these listed devices and *NEC* 110.3(B).

Various types of combiners such as source circuit combiners and re-combiners and other types of dc combiners have been combined into one definition – **Direct-Current (dc) Combiner**.

A **Multimode Inverter** is defined and this device will be appearing in the ever-increasing numbers of battery-backed-up, utility-interactive systems.

690.4 General Requirements. The identification and grouping requirements have been moved to section 690.31. DC-to-DC converters have been added to the listed equipment requirement. Bipolar PV systems are required to have a warning concerning overvoltage on equipment if the grounded conductors are disconnected.

690.5 Ground Fault Protection. These devices are now required to recognize ground faults in intentionally grounded conductors, and they are now required to be listed.

690.7 Maximum Voltage. The 600 V limit in one- and two-family dwellings remains, but the 600 volt maximum has been increased to 1000 volts in other installations.

For energy storage devices, significant details on the requirements for disconnects and overcurrent protection have been added.

690.9 Overcurrent Protection. Circuits connected to current-limited sources such as PV modules and utility-interactive inverters shall be protected from over currents at the source of those overcurrents – usually external sources. The rating of overcurrent devices now must consider terminal temperature requirements and operation in environments over 40° C. Overcurrent devices listed for PV applications shall be required in the dc PV circuits. In ungrounded PV arrays, overcurrent protection must be installed in each undergrounded conductor where circuit overcurrent protection is required.

Transformers connected to the output of utility interactive inverters with a rating the same as the utility interactive inverter are not required to have overcurrent protection from the inverter output.

690.12. Rapid Shutdown of PV Systems on Buildings. This new section requires a shutdown system that is to be used by first responders/Fire Service personnel that can shut down all PV circuits on or in a building within 10 seconds of activation. The controlled conductors after the shutdown must not have any more than 30 V or 240 VA between any two conductors and any conductor and ground. Energized conductor lengths inside the building will be limited to 1.5 m (5 feet) and no more than 3 m (10 feet) from the PV array outside the building,

Specific implementation details are not included in the *Code*. However, we can expect that the remote disconnect will be in a readily accessible location, clearly marked on the outside of the building and will probably be near the existing utility revenue meter. Circuits that will be impacted include module outputs, string outputs, combiner outputs, inverter outputs, and the dc input circuits on inverters which may be energized for up to five minutes. Energy storage devices, such as batteries, associated with the PV system will also have to be disconnected.

Section III. Disconnecting Means. The contents of section 690.13, 690.14, 690.15 and 690.17 have been revised and merged with 690.14 removed. Most requirements remain the same. DC combiners located on the roofs of buildings will have a load break rated disconnecting means in the combiner or within 1.8 m (6 ft). The disconnect may be controlled remotely but must have a manual operation function.

690.17 Disconnect Type. PV disconnecting means can be power operable with a manual operation function. A number of specific disconnecting means are now shown in the *Code*.

690.31 Wiring Methods Permitted. Conductors and wiring that are part of a listed system are now acceptable.

Inverter outputs may no longer be grouped in the same raceway as the PV source or PV output circuits unless there is a partition in the raceway (photo J-1).

Single conductor cables listed and labeled as PV cables or PV wire are permitted in cable trays even though they are not marked for CT use. They must be supported at intervals not to exceed 300 mm (12 in.) and must be secured at intervals not to exceed 1.4 m (4.5 in.).

Multi-conductor cables type TC ER or USE-2 may be permitted in outdoor locations connected to the output of PV inverters where the inverters are not mounted in readily accessible locations.

Additional requirements for markings on the dc PV circuits inside and outside of buildings has been added and specifications on the types of markings will be found in this section.

Significant portions of 690.4 regarding circuit routing and grouping have been transferred to this section.

690.35 Ungrounded Photovoltaic Power Systems. Ground Fault Protection. The ground fault protection equipment must now be listed.

690.41 System Grounding. The section has been revised to indicate grounding requirements for various types of systems.

690.45 Size of Equipment Grounding Conductors. Shortened due to the fact that all systems must have ground fault protection now.

PHOTO J-1 Those raceways must have an internal partition to separate dc PV source conductors from ac inverter output conductors

Appendix J — A Brief Overview

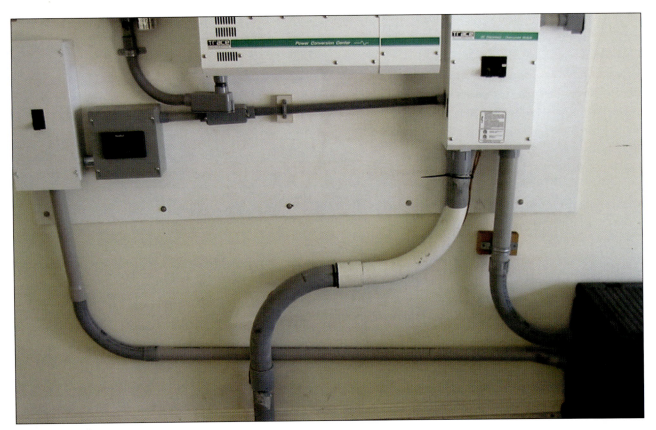

PHOTO J-2 Battery disconnect adjacent to battery enclosure.

690.47 Grounding Electrode System. (B) Direct-Current Systems. The AC equipment grounding system may now be used to provide equipment grounding for ungrounded dc systems.

690.47(D) Additional Auxiliary Electrodes for Array Grounding. This section returns from the 2008 *Code* after being removed from the 2011 *Code* and now has slight modifications for clarity.

690.53 Direct Current Photovoltaic Power Source. Systems with multiple dc outputs shall have the output currents marked for each of the outputs.

690 Part VIII. Storage batteries. 690.71 Installation. (H) Disconnection Overcurrent Protection. This new section establishes a number of significant requirements for disconnecting means and overcurrent protection for battery circuit output conductors (photo J-2).

690 Part IX. Systems over 1000 V. This section has been revised from 600 V to 1000 V and a section 690.81 has been added indicating that listed products should be installed in accordance with the listing.

690 Part X. Electric Vehicle Charging. This section primarily prefers to other sections of *Code* dealing with electric vehicle charging.

Article 705

Section **705.12 D** has had numerous revisions that will clarify previous code requirements and change several relating to the point of connection for utility interactive inverters on the load side of the service disconnect. See Appendix H for the full details of this section. (photo J-3).

705.12(D)(3)(d) allows connections to multi-ampacity bus works and center tapped panel boards where designed under engineering supervision that includes fault studies and busbar load calculations.

705.12(D)(6) will require listed AC AFCI protection for utility-interactive inverter outputs using exposed wire harnesses or cable operating at 240 V, 30 A, or less.

PHOTO J-3 Clarifications coming for load side connections

705.31 Location of Overcurrent Protection. This new section requires that the overcurrent protection for conductors for a supply-side utility interactive inverter connection be at the point of interconnection or within 3 m (10 ft) of that point.

705.100 Unbalanced Interconnections. (A) Single Phase. Single-phase inverters connected to three-phase power systems shall not result in unbalanced voltages exceeding 3%.

Appendix J — A Brief Overview

Index

Symbols

15-minute inspections 116
125 percent factor 33

A

Alternating current (ac) 18, 75, 96, 124, 131
    Connection 108
    Output circuit 23, 53, 68, 70, 124, 125
    Utility-connection 76
    Voltages 14
Ampacity 24, 28, 48, 53
    Temperature Correction 48
Arc-fault circuit interrupter 62, 65, 70, 100
Arcs 65
Array output 29
    Grounding 41
Arrays 29, 40, 43, 49, 51, 58, 52, 77, 143, 154
    Grounding 41, 45, 73, 77
    Output 29, 105
    Power rating 77
Authority having jurisdiction (AHJ) 19, 143, 154

B

Battery
    Banks 20, 23
    Currents 131
    Flow 12
    Storage 19
Bonding 38, 42
Breakers 70, 71, 81
Busbars 52, 85, 91, 93, 136, 150

C

Cables 36, 43, 53, 58, 97, 105, 113, 132, 145
    NM cable 59, 71
Changes and Challenges 11
Checklist, Inspector/Installer 143
Circuit 22, 33, 58, 64, 67, 77, 79, 92, 137
    Anti-islanding 67, 80
    Branch circuits 13, 33, 68, 101, 123
    Circuit breaker 23, 40, 64, 69, 70, 80, 83, 87, 104
    Continuous current 97, 108, 125
    Dedicated 14, 68, 101
    Feeder 26, 33
    General-purpose circuits 12
    Load 13
    Open circuit voltage 28, 30, 32
    Short-circuit current 28, 31
    Ungrounded 137
Circuit breakers 24, 71
Combiner 23, 52
Conductors 24, 36, 43, 46, 48, 52, 53, 57, 61, 77, 85, 87, 93, 124, 127, 129, 130, 132, 135, 137, 143
    Converters 96, 159
    Equipment Grounding 52, 60, 62, 143, 146, 154, 160
    Insulation 44
    Output 72, 82, 88, 106
    Service-entrance 87–91, 108
    Sizing 107, 130, 136
    Tap 85, 91
    Ungrounded 57, 94, 114, 137, 146
Conduits 43–48, 105, 113
Continuing education 15
Converters 96
    DC-to-DC converters 14, 22, 96, 100, 101, 159
Copper conductors 36, 41, 127, 127
Currents 18, 72, 80, 82, 87, 90, 123, 131
    Maximum 26
    Rating 130
    Short-circuit current 28, 31, 50, 65, 120, 131
    Sources 23
    Sunlight 29
    Surge 72, 76, 92, 123, 131
    Zero current 65

D

Direct current (dc) 13, 18, 25, 34, 53, 61, 75, 105, 130
    DC input fusing 61
    Disconnecting means 47, 50, 53
    Output circuits, 68
    Power distribution systems 14
    Voltages 14, 34
Disconnects 52, 59, 60, 68, 87, 90, 99, 105, 111, 113, 123
    AC disconnect 58, 98, 107, 111, 124
    DC disconnect 53, 58, 105, 107
    Main 91, 93
    Service 88, 91

E

Electrical inspectors 14, 33, 103
Electrical metallic tubing (EMT) 52
Electric vehicles 11
    Battery bank 11
    Hybrid 11
    Plug-in 11
    Pure electric cars 11
Electrode terminal 73, 76, 96, 123
Energy
    Demands 12
    Energy crisis 14, 18
    Renewable energy systems 14
Storage systems, large 11, 12
Equipment-grounding conductor 38, 52, 62, 122, 125

F

Fuel cell 13
Fuse 24, 52, 56, 89, 104, 137, 140

G

Generators 12, 61
    Backup 12
Ground-fault detection/interruption device (GFID) 26
Ground-fault protection 60, 61, 70, 96, 107, 111, 157
    Ground-fault circuit interrupters (GFCI) 61, 69, 101, 124
    Ground-fault protection devices (GFPD) 61, 107
Grounding 36, 37, 39, 60, 72, 111, 122, 146, 157
    AC grounding 75, 122, 125
    Array 40, 41, 43, 77
    Connections 73
    DC ground faults 60
    DC grounding 73, 76, 105
    Equipment grounding 52, 60, 76, 90, 122
    Instructions and consistency 37
    System 36, 72, 96, 122, 146, 157

H

Hardware
    Galvanized 43
    Stainless Steel 40, 43

I

Inspectors 14, 24, 27, 33, 37, 57, 81, 98, 103, 111, 116
Interactive power sources 11
Inverters 14, 19, 25, 31, 57, 58, 60, 68, 73, 79, 93, 96, 107, 111, 113, 122, 135, 137, 145
    Multiple 83, 92, 161
    Output circuit 72, 79, 88, 92, 107, 122
    Utility-interactive 21, 24, 30, 56, 59, 63, 66, 70, 72, 73, 77, 80, 84, 92, 96, 107, 125, 131, 138, 140, 148, 162

L

Lightning protection 42, 46, 77
Load-side connection 80, 85, 135
Luminaires
    Direct current 13

M

Maintenance disconnects 56, 59
Math 118
    Calculating module open-circuit voltage 120
    Expected lowest temperatures 119
    Millivolt Coefficients 119
    Module Short-Circuit Current 118
    Percentage coefficients 119
    Voltage Drop 120
Microinverter 77, 92, 96, 100, 122
    AC input and output cables 96, 97, 98, 122, 125
    AC output circuits 124
    Connectors 93, 122
    DC connection 100, 101
    Disconnects 123
    Grounding 97, 122
    Wiring 122
Modules 14, 18, 22, 26, 27, 33, 36, 40, 43, 94, 98, 101, 112, 122, 124, 137
    AC PV module 14, 68, 96, 98, 101, 122, 124
    Aluminum frames 22, 36, 46, 127
    DC connected 98, 137
    Grounding 36, 111, 122, 123
    IV Curve 28, 29
    Metal-framed 36, 127
    Multiple 135, 138
    Output voltage 26, 28, 30, 50, 67, 98, 131
    Power 34

N

National Electrical Code (NEC) 14, 18, 30, 61, 137

O

Open circuit voltage 33
Original equipment manufacturers (OEM) 38, 39
Overcurrent devices 11, 23, 30, 33, 50, 82, 105, 118, 130, 132, 135, 144
    Inverter 105, 107
    Ratings 131, 132, 135

P

Peak power 29, 65, 120
Photovoltaic (PV) power systems 11, 43, 103, 143, 154
    AC PV modules 14, 18, 22, 68
    Checklist 143
    Commercial systems 18, 19, 50, 70, 82, 90, 130
    Disconnect 49, 52
    Overview 18
    Power flows 54, 93
    Residential systems 19, 49, 72, 81, 90, 104, 130
    Stand-alone (off grid) 20
    Utility-interactive (grid-connected) 19, 120, 131, 137
Plan reviewers 14, 26, 100, 148, 153
    Plan check 103
Power distribution systems 13
Power purchase agreements (PPA) 14
PV combiners (PV j-boxes or PV combining enclosures) 23, 116, 130

Q

Qualified persons 14

R

Racks, Mechanical 40, 41
Renewable Energy Systems 14
Roofing 22, 43, 46, 61

S

Safety standards 15
Shock 30, 36, 61, 124, 127
Smart grid 12
Smart house 13
Smart meter 13
Source-circuit combiner 49
Standalone systems 20
Sunlight intensity 26, 29, 65
Supply-side utility connections 85, 87

T

Temperature limitations 52, 132
Transformer 11, 61, 70, 159

U

UL Standard 1703, Flat-Plate Photovoltaic Modules and Panels 30, 32, 37, 41, 127, 137, 143
UL Standard 1741, Inverters, Converters, Controllers and Interconnection System Equipment 23, 52, 73, 78, 123, 145
Underwriters Laboratories 15, 20, 30, 36, 127
Utility 11, 12, 25, 63, 79, 82
Utility-Interactive (U-I) PV systems 11, 18, 19, 25, 29, 36, 43, 58, 61, 70
    Turn off electricity from 29

V

Voltage drop 80, 120
    Calculating 118
Voltmeter 28

W

Wind power
    Systems 14
Wire 44, 57, 69, 105
    Field-installed 45
    USE-2 or PV Wire 44
Wiring methods 46, 58, 160

Index

Photovoltaic Power Systems for Inspectors, Plan Reviewers & Installers

Second Edition

Author: *John Wiles*

Editor in Chief: *David Clements*

Managing Editor: *Kathryn Ingley*

Technical Editor: *Keith Lofland*

Designer: *John Watson*

Project Manager: *Laura Hildreth*

Technical Reviewers

Keith Lofland

Director of Education, Codes and Standards, IAEI, Richardson, Texas

Rhonda Parkhurst

Building Inspector, City of Palo Alto, California

James J. Rogers

Principal Representative for IAEI on Code-Making Panel 4; Electrical Inspector, Towns of Oak Bluffs, Tisbury, West Tisbury, MA

Composed at International Association of Electrical Inspectors in Palatino LT Std, Arial and Garamond.
Printed by Walsworth Print Group on 70# Book. Bound in 12 pt. C1S Cover.